Churn to Enjoy Bliss, Stability and a Heavenly Life

(includes Brahma Kumaris Murli Extracts with Explanations)

Written by:

Brahma Kumari Pari

First Edition 2023
Copyright © 2023 by GBK Publications, Malaysia
Published by GBK Publications
Web-sites:
http://www.gbk-books.com (For List of Books)
http://www.brahmakumari.net (For articles which can be read for free)

Table of Contents

Chapter 1: Introduction

When BKs deeply contemplate on the BK knowledge, it is said that they are churning the knowledge. A BK is a spiritual effort maker who makes spiritual efforts based on the 'knowledge given by God in the Brahma Kumaris'. This knowledge is also referred to as:

1. Gyan (which means knowledge), or

2. BK Knowledge.

This knowledge can be found in the murlis (God's messages/teachings) which God has spoken in the Brahma Kumaris.

Around 1936, God came into the Corporeal World, and began giving Lekhraj visions and guidance. With time:

1. BKs began to refer to Lekhraj as Brahma Baba.

2. God began using the physical body of Brahma Baba to give knowledge for 'world transformation through self-transformation'. Therefore, as we transform into the divine state, through contemplating/churning on the knowledge given by God, the world also transforms into the Golden Aged world.

The sakar murlis are those which were spoken by God through using the physical body of Brahma Baba. When Brahma Baba left his physical body, he began to play his avyakt/angelic role, and God continued to use Brahma Baba's angelic body for world service. The avyakt murlis are God's messages/teachings that were spoken through using avyakt Brahma Baba and the physical body of Dadi Gulzar.

Since the BK knowledge is given by God, you are remembering God when you churn (contemplate on) this knowledge. This is why BKs are involved with churning the BK knowledge. You are also churning the knowledge when you remember God (the Supreme Soul) based on the knowledge that has been given by God in the murlis. You establish and maintain your direct link to God through churning (contemplating on) the BK knowledge.

In the murlis, God has given knowledge on the soul, Supreme Soul, Cycle of Time, etc. It is essential to churn/contemplate on these in order to become spiritually powerful. You receive multimillion-fold benefits through this churning process. Before I give further explanations on the benefits received, let me first briefly explain about the soul, Supreme Soul, Cycle of Time, etc so that you will have a better understanding on what is being explained in this book.

Each one of us is a soul (a point of metaphysical white light). We are not our bodies; we are using our bodies to live our lives. The original qualities of the soul are the virtues and powers. The virtues are good qualities such as peace, love, happiness, etc. BKs practice the meditation called Brahma Kumaris Raja Yoga so as to:

1. absorb divine virtues and powers from God through their link to God.

2. transform their virtues and powers (which are in the ordinary state) into divine virtues and powers through being empowered by God's vibrations which are absorbed through their link to God.

3. transform the vices into virtues and powers through exposure of the vices to God's powerful Light. The vices include anger, greed, ego etc.

God is also a metaphysical Point of Light. However, among all souls, God is the Supreme because he has the spiritual strength of an Ocean while we are like a drop in comparison. For this reason, God is the Supreme Soul (Paramatma). The Supreme Soul is the spiritual Father of all human souls. Moreover, during the Confluence Age, we also have an additional Father-child relationship with Him. Hence, BKs refer to God as Baba (Father).

God is the Ocean of Love, Ocean of Happiness, Ocean of Bliss, Ocean of Peace etc because He is the Ocean of all Divine Virtues and Powers. Since you get linked to God through churning the knowledge, you will be able to absorb these Divine Virtues and Powers from God to empower yourself. Through empowering yourself, you enjoy bliss, stability, etc.

In the murlis, God has said that time flows in a cyclic manner. Each Cycle of Time (hereafter referred to as the Cycle) consists of the following five Ages:

1. Satyuga (Golden Age),

2. Tretayuga (Silver Age),

3. Dwapuryuga (Copper Age),

4. Kaliyuga (Iron Age), and

5. Sangamyuga (Confluence Age).

During the first half cycle (which consists of the Golden and Silver Ages):

1. Mankind lives in a divine world.

2. the people live a heavenly life, as deities. The souls, who take births in the first half cycle, are referred to as deity souls.

Then, the world transforms into the ordinary state, at the end of the Silver Age. Therefore, Mankind lives in an ordinary world during the second half cycle (which is from the beginning of the Copper Age until the end of the Iron Age). Finally, around the end of the Iron Age, God comes into the Corporeal World to transform the world into the Golden Aged world again. This transformation process takes place during the Confluence Age which overlaps:

1. the ending phase of Kaliyuga, and

2. the beginning phase of Satyuga.

The Confluence Age began around 1936 when God (the Supreme Soul) came into the Corporeal World, from the Soul World.

The Soul World is the Home of God and all human souls. We (the souls) left the Soul World and came into the Corporeal World to play our parts in the World Drama on earth. The same World Drama repeats during every Cycle. We play our parts on earth, through using physical bodies, as per this predestined World Drama. God does not leave the Soul World to take births in the Corporeal World like how human souls do. God only comes into the Corporeal World, at the end of each Cycle, so as to:

1. purify souls and take them back to the Soul World.

2. transform the world into the Golden Aged world and bring in the next Cycle.

While God is on His way to the Corporeal World, He creates the Angelic World (which is also referred to as the Subtle Region). This Angelic World:

1. exists between the Soul World and Corporeal World.

2. only exists during the Confluence Age.

When we churn the knowledge, we bring ourselves into the Angelic World because God has enabled us to do this through churning the knowledge and remembering Him. While we are in the Angelic World, we use our angelic body. We (the souls) do not completely leave our physical body to use our angelic body which is in the Angelic World. Basically, we are using two worlds (Corporeal World and Angelic World) at the same time, when we are in the Confluence Age.

When one is introduced to the BK knowledge, some of the energies of the soul fly to the Angelic World to remain there. This keeps one in the Confluence Age. Then, when one makes spiritual efforts, more of the energies of the soul fly to the Angelic World to establish a strong link to God who is also residing in the Subtle Region during the Confluence Age. One is in the **angelic stage** when one's link to God is strong. Since one's energies are in the Angelic World:

1. one is residing in the Angelic World, and

2. one's consciousness is in the Angelic World while one uses one's physical body in the Corporeal World.

When you churn this knowledge, have faith that you are in the Confluence Age because this faith helps to keep you:

1. in the Confluence Age.

2. linked to God.

For so long as you are remembering God and churning the BK knowledge, you will remain in the Confluence Age and become spiritually more powerful. More on churning the knowledge can be found further below and in the chapters of this book.

In the Kaliyug world, all human souls (who are in the Corporeal World) are in a spiritually weak state because:

1. from the beginning of the Golden Age, souls were gradually losing spiritual energy, to become spiritually weaker, as they played their parts on earth.

2. from the beginning of the Copper Age, souls were indulging in the vices to become impure. The souls were becoming spiritually weaker more quickly since they were indulging in the vices.

Since human souls are in a very weak impure state by the end of Kaliyuga, God has to come, at the end of each Cycle, to re-energise us to become pure and spiritually powerful. Thus, after having come into the Corporeal World, God gives us the murlis so that we can churn the knowledge to get linked to God. Through churning the BK knowledge, we receive multimillion-fold benefits; some of these benefits are the following:

1. we enjoy God's Company now.

2. we become spiritually powerful. Thus, our stability increases.

3. we get closer and closer to God as we become spiritually powerful.

4. we experience intoxicating bliss through being linked to God.

5. our virtues and powers increase. Hence, we can enjoy greater happiness, peace, bliss, etc now and in our future births.

6. we become victorious over the vices with God's assistance. Therefore, we will not be troubled by the vices. We will be able to

overcome all the challenges, which the vices throw in our way, through just contemplating on the BK knowledge.

7. we can easily get God's love, help and guidance since we have a link to God. The stronger the link, the easier it is to get His help.

8. we have various kinds of blissful experiences.

9. we transform into the divine state. So we regain our perfect Golden Aged world where we can enjoy divine happiness, status, wealth etc.

10. we will have a better understanding on the BK knowledge. In the murlis, Baba keeps telling us to churn because we have to do this to understand the knowledge which can be found in the murlis. We have a better understanding when we accumulate more 'jewels of knowledge' through our link to God. Baba refers to the knowledge, which has been given by Him, as the 'jewels of knowledge' because the more we accumulate this knowledge, the more we enjoy the benefits. There are more explanations in Chapter 12 (Jewels of Knowledge and Pilgrimage of Remembrance) on why this knowledge is referred to as the 'jewels of knowledge'.

As you read this book, you will have a better understanding on the benefits received through the churning process. This 'understanding' improves when you have experiences through churning the knowledge.

In the Hindu scriptures, there is a myth which is referred to as Samudra Manthan or 'Churning the Ocean of Milk'. This myth was created by the deity souls, after the last Silver Age:

1. since they had lost their divine world.

2. based on memories that were emerging in respect of what happens during the Confluence Age.

In this myth, the ocean is churned to extract amrit (nectar of immortality). As they churn, other valuables also emerge from the ocean; amrit/nectar is the last of the treasures which emerge from the churning of the ocean. The Hindu texts portray amrit as a sweet drink/elixir which grants the Devas immortality when they consume it. In truth, this amrit is drunk by the deity souls at the end of each Cycle of Time when the creation of the new Golden Aged world takes place through the Confluence Age. Those who drink it enjoy immortality when they live as deities in the Golden and Silver Ages.

In this Hindu myth, the ocean of milk was portrayed as being churned at the beginning of creation because:

1. the deity souls remembered what had happened while they were churning the BK knowledge, during the previous Confluence Age, on the creation of the Golden Age, etc. It should be noted that the BK knowledge is referred to as the milk of knowledge and the Golden Age is referred to as the ocean of milk, in the murlis. During the previous Confluence Age, while these deity souls were churning the milk of knowledge, they were also having desirable experiences of being in the ocean of milk.

2. the deity souls wanted to remain connected to their divine heavenly world (since they were not happy that they had lost their divine world).

3. the deity souls wanted to see the recreation of their Golden Aged world. During the previous Confluence Age, they had seen that the Golden Age was brought into existence through their churning. Thus, they knew that the Golden Aged world can be created through that churning.

4. the deity souls were waiting for the day when they could drink amrit again to regain immortality.

Hence, based on memories, this myth was created as a memorial of what happens during the Confluence Age. As portrayed in this myth, we receive a lot of benefits through churning the knowledge. However, the main aim (the greatest benefit) is extracting and drinking nectar so as to enjoy immortality in the Golden Age (ocean of milk). Through churning the knowledge, you are extracting nectar and drinking it because:

1. you are absorbing God's powerful Divine Virtues and Powers which are so sweet and intoxicating.

2. the soul's light is transforming into the sweet divine state as you absorb God's Light. Since your virtues and powers are also transforming into divine virtues and powers, you are accumulating more nectar that enables you to experience bliss when they are in an emerged state.

3. you are accumulating blissful experiences due to being filled with God's divine vibrations. These experiences, which are stored within the soul, are like nectar since they enable you to easily experience the sweet divine stage again when they emerge.

4. you experience the soul conscious stage, i.e. you experience yourself as the pure, virtuous, powerful soul. During the Confluence Age, you are soul conscious when you are in a spiritually high stage. Then, during the Golden and Silver Ages, you constantly remain soul conscious because you acquired this ability during the previous Confluence Age.

5. you are gaining the ability to live in the Golden Age where you enjoy immortality, i.e. you are now acquiring immortality through the churning process.

6. as you transform, your world is also transforming into the divine Golden Aged world where only deities can live. In the Golden Age, you can only experience divine happiness, peace, abundance and all other lovely stuff. The vices do not exist in the Golden Age.

7. you are receiving numerous other enjoyable benefits too due to being assisted by God now. Some of these have been listed out earlier on.

As you churn the knowledge, you get linked to the Ocean of Knowledge (God) and you are also transforming into the divine state so that you can enjoy all the benefits of living in the ocean of milk (Golden Age). The Golden Age is like an ocean of milk because everything, which exists in it, nourishes the human beings who live there as deities. Further, during the Golden and Silver Ages, the weaker deity souls and everything else are sustained by the powerful deity souls who were energised by God during the previous Confluence Age. This ocean of milk is getting created as we churn the BK knowledge (milk of knowledge), now. This knowledge is like milk that nourishes us because:

1. God's Sounds of Silence accompany the knowledge.

2. the knowledge links us to God and enables us to absorb God's vibrations which nourishes us further.

Hence, when we churn the knowledge, it is as if we are churning milk. The churning enables us to grow spiritually so that we take our next birth in the ocean of milk (Golden Age). We can also have experiences of being in the ocean of milk, now, when we churn the milk of knowledge. More on the milk of knowledge can be found in Chapter 8 (Milk of Knowledge).

In the Hindu myths, Krishna is portrayed as enjoying the butter that has been extracted from milk. Extracting the butter from the milk and enjoying this butter has the same significance as extracting nectar and drinking it, i.e. it refers to receiving all the abovementioned benefits through churning the knowledge. When you churn the knowledge, you extract butter (the benefits) because you are exposed to the light of the Ocean of Knowledge (God) through the churning process, i.e. you are extracting the butter since you are energised by God's Light when you churn.

When we are in a high stage, all our energies are in the pure divine state; in addition, a little of our energies permanently transform into the divine state. When we lose our high stage:

1. all our energies, which have temporarily been empowered to become divine, lose their divine state to become ordinary again, and

2. our energies, which have permanently transformed into the divine state, will go deeper within. If we emerge them through a thought, we attain a high stage again.

All the energies, which have permanently transformed into the divine state, are also amrit or butter which keep emerging to remain on the surface of the soul whenever we remember Baba and churn the knowledge. We must keep remembering Baba and churning the knowledge, until all our energies permanently transform into the divine state; when we do this, we are extracting and drinking amrit/butter.

Further, when a deity soul entertained a vice, at the end of the Silver Age, our divine self (along with all the divine virtues and powers) sank deep within into the soul. Now, when we churn this knowledge, the divine virtues and powers (which had sunk deep into the soul at the end of the Silver Age) emerge because we are being transformed back into the divine state through the churning process. These divine virtues and powers are also nectar/amrit or butter that emerges through the churning process. We experience the sweet taste of nectar when they are in an emerged state. Since the deity souls have these divine virtues and powers deep within them, they have an inherent ability to transform back into the divine state. When they regain their spiritual strength, through exposure to God's vibrations, the deity souls transform back into the divine state. We have to keep 'extracting and consuming' the amrit/nectar or butter, through the churning process, until we completely transform into the divine state.

Churning the knowledge enables us to imbibe the knowledge. As we imbibe, we are extracting and consuming the amrit/nectar or butter. When we are saturated with knowledge (as we are when we are churning), we will have a strong link to God. Hence, we can get a better understanding on the knowledge from Baba. We are also extracting and enjoying amrit/nectar or butter when this happens.

We are fortunate that God has given us the knowledge in the murlis so that we can churn to extract nectar/butter. One of the most crucial points to churn on, so as to extract the nectar/butter, is that each one of us is a soul because this:

1. brings us out of the body conscious state.

2. enables us to enjoy the soul conscious stage.

The body conscious state is the weak ordinary state where we feel that we are the body. When we are in the body conscious state, the pure light of the soul can transform into the impure state when we indulge in the vices.

During the first half cycle (in the Golden and Silver Ages), the deities enjoy immortality because they are soul conscious. Since they are in the soul conscious state, they are aware that they are the pure divine souls. It is only during the second half cycle (in the Copper and Iron Ages) that we are in the body conscious state. During the Confluence Age, we become soul conscious again through God's assistance, i.e. while we are exposed to God's vibrations, we are empowered to enjoy the soul conscious stage. During the soul conscious stage:

1. we are filled with God's vibrations. God's vibrations within us (the souls) are like nectar that enables us to enjoy the sweet, intoxicating, blissful stage. It can also be said that God's vibrations, which are within us (the souls), are like valuable butter. Just as butter makes the food which we eat tasty, God's vibrations make us feel good; our life and lifestyle will also be good, enabling us to experience happiness. Due to being filled with God's Light, we will experience sweetness when we are in the Confluence Age, Golden Age and Silver Age. The food which we eat will also taste so good since it is in the pure state.

2. our virtues and powers are all in the divine state. These divine virtues and powers will taste so sweet like nectar/amrit. The virtues and powers, which are in the ordinary state, will not taste like nectar. Hence, when the ordinary virtues and powers transform into the divine state, we are extracting nectar/butter (something valuable). Another reason why we are extracting butter when they transform is that they enable us to take our next birth as a deity in the Golden Age.

The soul conscious stage itself is like amrit because when we are in
the soul conscious stage:

1. all the energies of the soul will be in the sweet divine state.

2. we experience bliss.

3. we gain the ability to enjoy immortality during the Golden and
Silver Ages (where the world of the deities exists). All deity souls will
enjoy immortality during the first half cycle because we drink nectar
now through churning the knowledge.

Through attaining the soul conscious stage now, via constantly
remembering Baba and churning the knowledge, we will constantly
remain soul conscious in our lives during the Golden and Silver Ages.
Since we are acquiring the ability to remain in the soul conscious stage
now, we have to be given the Golden Aged world to live in.

In order to help us attain the soul conscious stage, God relates the
knowledge to the souls; we (the souls) subtly listen to God when we
read or listen to the murli. Since God empowers us as we listen/read:

1. we (the souls) are seated on our seat which is in the center of the
forehead.

2. we are soul conscious.

It should be noted that whenever we are seated on our seat, we are
soul conscious. When we are in the powerful soul conscious stage, we
are aware that we are the souls and not the body.

You can also sit on your seat, in the center of your forehead, when
you contemplate/churn on a murli point (point of knowledge that is
from a murli). You can churn on a murli point which is:

1. from the murli that was read on that day in the BK centers,

2. from any of Baba's murlis, or

3. from a murli extract in this book (see the chapters which has
murli extracts with further explanations below it).

When you churn a murli point, you should recollect what you had
heard in all the earlier murlis so as to understand what is being said
in the murli point. For example, when you churn a murli point on the

soul, you can think about all the BK knowledge relating to the soul; this means that you can contemplate on:

1. the eternal form of the soul as a point of light.

2. how the soul's original qualities are the virtues and powers.

3. how all human souls are the children of God (the Supreme Soul).

4. how the soul leaves the Soul World and comes to play its part in the World Drama on earth.

5. how God is empowering the souls now (during the Confluence Age), to take them back to the Soul World.

6. how the deity souls are transforming back into the divine state during the Confluence Age.

7. how the soul takes many births during each Cycle of Time, etc.

While remembering that you are the soul and not the body, have the feeling that you are the soul who is in the soul conscious stage. Sustain this feeling, with faith, so that you soak yourself up with this knowledge because this will enable you to experience it in a practical way.

You should begin your spiritual effort making through seeing yourself as a pure, virtuous soul. When you see yourself as the soul, you are churning the knowledge because you see yourself as the soul based on the BK knowledge. Therefore, you absorb/imbibe this knowledge and become soul conscious. Actually, you can become soul conscious through churning on any murli point. As you imbibe the knowledge which you are churning on, you:

1. will have a relevant blissful experience, and

2. become soul conscious.

If your spiritual stage is not good when you begin churning the knowledge, you will initially go into the initial stage of absorption. Then, as you keep churning the knowledge, you go into the final stage of absorption and experience yourself as the blissful soul. When you keep churning, while you are in a high spiritual stage, you remain in the final stage; so you maintain a high stage.

Since murli points (along with explanations) are provided in this book, you can easily attain and remain in the powerful soul conscious stage through churning on the contents in this book. When you are soul conscious, you will be in control of yourself because you will be using the faculties of the soul in an accurate manner. This is also one of the benefits received through churning the knowledge.

The soul has three faculties: mind, intellect and memory bank (sanskaras). The soul uses the mind, intellect and sanskaras as it lives its life on earth. The mind, intellect and memory bank also get filled with this powerful knowledge when you churn the knowledge; due to this:

1. you absorb the knowledge and God's Power of Silence (which accompany the knowledge) to attain a high spiritual stage.

2. the mind, intellect and sanskaras are energised through being exposed to God's Light. This enables them to work efficient. This is also a reason why you have control over them and yourself.

It should be noted that while you contemplate on the knowledge, you use the intellect to churn the knowledge like how an instrument is used to churn milk in order to get the highly valued butter. Therefore, when you churn the knowledge, your intellect is:

1. filled with the knowledge, and

2. exposed to God's Sounds of Silence that accompany the knowledge.

Due to the above, your intellect gets energised (by God's Light) to become divine. The divine intellect has the ability to link you to God who is the Ocean of Knowledge. Hence, your intellect links you to God and you are directly exposed of God's powerful Light. Since God's Sounds of Silence accompany the knowledge, you are getting God's assistance to extract butter/amrit and enjoy the taste of butter/amrit. There are more explanations on God's Sounds of Silence in the chapters of this book.

In the Kaliyug world, one uses the left hemisphere of the brain to act in an intelligent manner; while doing this, one is capable of indulging in the vices since one is in the ordinary state. Thus, a person might act like he is superior to all others, etc. This will turn the others away from, or against, him. Life can be very difficult for him, as a result. Further, since the intellect is in an ordinary state, it cannot be used efficiently to enable him to make wise decisions, etc. The ordinary intellect can easily make him feel confused. As a consequence, he can make a lot of wrong moves etc that can mess up his life.

One who churns the BK knowledge (a spiritual effort maker):

1. will be getting God's help.

2. can only be very simple and angelic since the soul will only be filled with divine virtues and powers when the spiritual stage is high.

3. will be using the divine intellect. It should be borne in mind that a divine intellect can be used efficiently.

4. uses the right hemisphere more than the left. Thus, one can easily experience a light spiritual state.

5. will have complete control over oneself since one will have complete control over one's mind, intellect and sanskaras when the stage is high.

6. will be making accurate decisions.

One will be making accurate decisions, when one's stage is high, because:

1. one will be using the divine intellect.

2. one will be getting God's assistance to do the right thing.

3. one will know what to do and how to conduct oneself since one has the knowledge.

Due to all the above, while you are a spiritual effort maker, you can act in a wise, accurate manner. In addition, all the above and your 'pure powerful stage' will attract others to you and enable you to live a happier, peaceful, more fulfilling life. You can actually live a heavenly, blissful life now itself since you are becoming divine and have God's Company. For all these reasons, churn the knowledge as much as possible to improve the quality of your life now and in your future births.

The mind, intellect and memory bank (sanskaras) are explained further in the chapters of this book. You have to churn the knowledge in these chapters so as to understand how the soul uses the mind, intellect and sanskaras. Since this knowledge on the mind, intellect and sanskaras is BK knowledge, you attain a high stage through this churning.

BKs churn this knowledge for 'world transformation through self-transformation'. This means that:

1. they churn the knowledge to become spiritually powerful and transform into the divine state, and

2. as they transform, the world also transforms into the Golden Aged world.

For this transformation to take place, we must also have the aim to remain surrendered to God through following His teachings in the murlis. When we churn the knowledge with the abovementioned intentions, we are like 'moths' who fly towards the Light/Flame (God) so as to completely surrender to the Light/Flame/God. Since we are still using the old bodies to make spiritual efforts, we are like the moths. At the same time, when we churn the knowledge, we are transforming to become like beautiful butterflies which will live in the ocean of milk (Golden Age) due to having been submerged in the ocean of knowledge during the Confluence Age; it is like we will emerge from the ocean of knowledge as beautiful butterflies so as to live in the ocean of milk (Golden Age). We will be like beautiful butterflies, while we are in the ocean of milk (Golden Age), because:

1. we will have pure, perfect, beautiful bodies, and

2. we will be in the lovely, divine state.

During the Confluence Age, we are submerged in the ocean of knowledge when we intensely churn the knowledge because:

1. we are saturated with knowledge.

2. the knowledge links us to the Ocean of Knowledge. As a consequence, we are also linked to the ocean of knowledge that is within God. Through the link, we receive more knowledge, so as to have a further understanding on the knowledge; hence, we get saturated with the knowledge further.

3. God's magical Sounds of Silence accompany the knowledge that is given by Him. So we are submerged in these and, through these Sounds of Silence, we are connected to the ocean of knowledge which is within God. When we understand the knowledge, through this connection, we are saturated with more knowledge.

More explanations on the 'ocean of knowledge' can be found in Chapter 7 (Churn the Ocean of Knowledge).

There are many BKs who are just churning the knowledge because they want to experience happiness now, in this birth. They are interested in becoming spiritually powerful so that they can be happy and not be burdened by problems. You can churn the knowledge for this reason too. However, always have the view:

1. that you are transforming into the Golden Aged state, i.e. have the aim to become a beautiful Golden Aged deity who is as lovely as a beautiful butterfly.

2. that the world is transforming into the Golden Aged state, as you transform.

When you have these views, you can easily enjoy the benefits that are received through the churning process, e.g. you become spiritually powerful and, as you become spiritually powerful, you will find it easier and easier to remain happy (without depending on external situations to experience happiness). Do not wonder about whether you and the world are transforming or not. Just have the view that you and the world are transforming so that you can enjoy all the benefits received through the churning process.

Further, when you are reading or listening to the murli, just read or listen to it without wondering about what Baba is trying to say in those sentences which you do not understand. Those sentences, which you do not understand, have to be explained to you by a senior BK. You will not be able to learn everything so quickly. Therefore, just read, or listen to, the murli without going into a state where you are questioning or are confused. When you begin to question, you might create too many thoughts and some of these might not be based on the BK knowledge. When you are in such a state, Maya (the vices) can easily emerge to topple you over. If you are not 'on guard', through keeping a check on your thoughts and feelings, you might lose your high stage. This practice of listening/reading, without going into negativity, will also help you to develop the habit of 'listening and watching whatever is happening around you, without going into negativity'.

When you churn, you should not have any thoughts that is not based on BK knowledge. The words in the murli should not be understood based on non-BK knowledge. Words, often have a different meaning in the BK knowledge. You have to keep reading, or listen to, further BK explanations so as to understand the meaning of the words. Accept what is being explained with faith (without questioning what is being said) because you will only enjoy the benefits of the churning when you have this faith and acceptance. It should be noted that through the churning process, you understand the Truth. The more you understand the Truth, the easier it will be to accept the knowledge. When you keep churning, the queue of question marks will end because:

1. God will be helping and guiding you.
2. you will be in the pure soul conscious stage.
3. you will know and accept the knowledge through experiences.

Therefore, there will not be any doubts about it. When you begin the churning process, make sure that you are in a virtuous state. Push all negative thoughts and bad emotions out of your mind. Emerge happiness into your mind; you emerge happiness into your mind by just feeling happy. You can also make sure that there is peace or some other virtue in your mind, when you begin making spiritual efforts. It is very difficult to establish a strong link to Baba when you are indulging in the vices, whereas it is very easy to establish and maintain a strong link to Baba when you are in the virtuous state. So keep trying your best to remain in a virtuous state so that you can easily remain strongly linked to God while you churn the knowledge.

If you are finding it difficult to begin meditation through attaining and maintaining a virtuous stage, turn your attention to what is being said in the knowledge. Through this:

1. you turn your attention away from your problems which are keeping the vices in an emerged state within your mind.

2. you turn your attention towards God, and the knowledge which He has given, so as to establish your link to God. When you are linked to Him, His Divine Virtues and Powers will be flowing into you to keep you in the pure, virtuous state. It should also be noted that when you are linked to God, God liberates you from the vices: the vices which are in an emerged state will be burnt away and the vices will also not be able to emerge when you are in a spiritually powerful stage.

As a result, it will be easy for you to continue making spiritual efforts. God has given you the knowledge so that you can use it as a powerful tool to help yourself.

There are murli extracts with explanations, in this book, so that you can churn the knowledge and enjoy all the benefits as you read this book. The explanations that have been given after each murli extract, in this book, will help you to understand what God is saying in the quoted murli extract. Therefore, you will find it easier to churn the murli points. These explanations also provide suggestions that can assist you during the churning process. The explanations for the murli extracts do not just focus on giving explanations based on the chapter title and murli extract because the explanations are for helping the reader to understand the knowledge on an overall basis. Further explanations are given so that:

1. you have a better understanding on the knowledge.

2. you can be taught on how to churn the knowledge in the murlis.

3. you can churn the BK knowledge in an accurate and efficient manner.

A proper understanding on the knowledge will help you to easily become an embodiment of knowledge, i.e. you will easily attain a spiritually powerful stage. Therefore, churn on all the knowledge that is in the chapters of this book; this will help you to enjoy all the benefits of the churning process. If you do not churn the knowledge to become an embodiment of knowledge, you will easily get filled with waste since you are not filled with God's Virtues and Powers as a consequence of being filled with God's knowledge.

When you churn the knowledge, which is in this book, you will easily establish your link to God and remain in yoga with God/Baba because you understand what you are reading (since relevant explanations are given in this book). As a result, you get filled with God's Virtues and Powers. Thus, read and contemplate on the quotes and explanations, in this book, to easily maintain a strong link to God. If you are new to BK Gyan, you should read the whole book to briefly know what is being said. Then, re-read one 'murli extract and its explanation' everyday so as to churn on it deeply.

As you keep churning the knowledge, your power of concentration increases because you are developing the habit to have fewer thoughts. When you have a developed power of concentration, you can instantly attain a high spiritual stage with just a thought. Hence, when you churn, you should keep trying to limit your thoughts to just one or a few murli points a day so as to:

1. improve your power of concentration.

2. develop the habit of thinking fewer thoughts.

However, you might find this difficult, and you might start looking around for something new to think about, if you have been thinking numerous thoughts for a long duration of time (before receiving BK

Gyan). To overcome this bad habit, think about different murli points until your power of concentration increases. This will make sure that your attention does not get turned to non-BK stuff due to a bad thinking habit; you can also turn your attention to BK pictures, BK songs, etc. However, try to just concentrate on one murli point per day, if it is possible, because this:

1. improves your power of concentration, and

2. enables you to have a lovely experience on it.

You can churn the knowledge through just one thought because, when you have that thought, you dive into the ocean of knowledge so as to have a better understanding on it, etc.

Actually, when you churn on one murli point, there can be so much to think about because you can think about everything that God has said about that murli point. I have already given an example earlier about how you can think on all the knowledge concerning the soul when you think about the soul. To make it clearer, I will give another example. In the murlis, Baba constantly tells us to remember Him. When you remember Him:

1. you can think about all that which I have said about God.

2. you can remember Him through churning on His attributes, as explained in the BK knowledge.

God's attributes include everything about Him, such as:

1. His Virtues and Powers,

2. what He does for human souls,

3. how He takes all human souls back Home to the Soul World,

4. how he recreates the Golden Aged world through giving us this knowledge, etc.

When you contemplate on God's attributes:

1. you get linked to Him.

2. you get re-charged as you get filled with His Virtues and Powers.

3. you will have a greater understanding on God.

4. you get closer to Him.

5. you can have an experience of being with Him in the Incorporeal World or Subtle Region, etc.

Consider yourself as being very fortunate to have been given this opportunity to have a relationship with God Himself through your power of yoga. At the same time, churn on all that which has been said about God, in depth. Keep remembering that Baba is actually a Point of Light. Just like how you will keep remembering everything about a person you love, keep remembering everything about Baba. When you churn on Baba's attributes, you are churning the knowledge. As a consequence, you understand and experience God from all the various angles; you also get closer to God. You have relevant experiences based on what you contemplate on, and you will also receive multimillion-fold benefits.

Digestion is necessary for the body to become and remain healthy. Similarly, churning the knowledge is necessary for the soul to become and remain healthy, i.e. to become and remain 'pure and powerful'. Through churning the knowledge:

1. you become an embodiment of experience.
2. you become spiritually powerful.
3. you enjoy bliss as you live your life.
4. your stability increases.

Therefore, you can easily remain Maya-proof and obstacle-proof so as to keep enjoying peace and happiness. Life can be so heavenly if you keep churning the BK knowledge.

The knowledge in this book is meant to guide you on how to become pure and spiritually powerful through the churning process. Since churning the knowledge keeps you in a pure state, you can easily enjoy bliss, stability and a heavenly life.

I have only briefly explained the Cycle of Time in this chapter. More explanations can be found in the other chapters of this book. It should be noted that when you keep the Cycle of Time in your mind as you churn on the various murli points, you can easily attain a very high stage and have blissful experiences. This will also help you to have a better understanding on the BK knowledge. So keep the Cycle of Time in your mind, as you read this book.

Chapter 2: Soul

When you begin churning the knowledge, always consider yourself as the soul who is using the body to churn the knowledge. This will immediately link you to God (our Father/Baba). When you keep churning the knowledge in this way:

1. you will understand what you are churning.

2. you will be able to enjoy all the benefits that are received through the churning.

The following murli extract, and the explanations below it, are on the soul. Keep churning on what is being said there so that you experience yourself as the pure soul. You attain the powerful soul conscious stage when you churn on it. While you are in the soul conscious stage, you know that you are the soul. When you keep experiencing yourself as the soul, you will find it easier to see yourself as the 'soul who is churning the knowledge' no matter which aspect of the knowledge you are churning on.

Further, as you keep experiencing yourself as the soul, you get filled with the divine virtues and powers, i.e. you keep accumulating treasures. This will help you to enjoy greater stability, bliss, etc. The more the treasures you accumulate through this churning process, the more heavenly a life you can live now and in the future. During the Confluence Age, your accumulated treasures will enable you to easily:

1. experience the accumulated divine virtues and powers as you live your life.

2. remain in God's Company. So God's Divine Virtues and Powers will keep flowing into you.

3. maintain an angelic stage as you do everything.

Therefore, life can be so heavenly. In the future, you will be living heavenly lives in the Golden and Silver Ages. So keep thinking about the following murli point and the explanations on it. When you keep thinking deeply about it, you are churning the knowledge.

"You now understand that we souls are invisible. It is the soul that has to study. It is the soul that does everything. ...Understand this very firmly: I am a soul. Baba is teaching us; I, a soul, am studying through this body. These are my *organs*. I, this soul, am separate from them. I act through these physical organs. I am not the physical organs. I, a soul, am separate from them. I have taken this body to play my *part;* this too, a spiritual part. No human beings, apart from you, can play this *part*. Repeatedly consider yourselves to be souls and remember the Father."

(Sakar Murli 31-7-20)

Explanations on the murli extract for churning:

One of the most important things in Brahma Kumaris Raja Yoga is to experience oneself as the soul. The soul is a tiny point of white light that is not visible with the physical eyes. Since you (the soul) are in your body, the body is alive. You (the soul) use your body to perform actions and even to make spiritual efforts. You have to firmly keep instilling it within you, every day, by repeatedly reminding yourself that you are the soul who is doing all the actions. Through this, you can easily attain the pure soul conscious stage. This is a reason why Baba/God keeps asking you to remember that you are the soul and not the body. Keep remembering that you are here to play your part in the World Drama and that you (the soul) are now playing your part in the Confluence Age with Baba. Through such thoughts, you (the soul) will easily attain the angelic stage.

Chapter 3: Supreme Soul (God)

When you remember God (our Father/Baba):

1. you can deeply think about something that has been said about Him in the murlis, or

2. you can deeply think about the various things which have been said about Him in the murlis.

When you think deeply about God, based on what has been said in the murlis, you are:

1. remembering Him, and

2. churning the knowledge.

In order to link yourself to God through the churning process, you have to:

1. know who God.

2. accept it that you are a soul and that God is the Supreme Soul.

The Supreme Soul is 'parlokik' because:

1. He is a metaphysical Point of Light,

2. He constantly resides in the Soul World which is beyond the Corporeal World, and

3. He does not have a physical body of His own, in the Corporeal World.

In His murlis, God has said that the most appropriate name for Him is 'Shiva'. Since He is the Father of souls, BKs refer to Him as Shiv Baba. What has been explained so far will enable you to briefly understand the following murli extract. More on God is provided in the murli extract and explanations which are further down. Since you have to know who God is in order to link yourself to Him, keep churning on the following murli extract and on the explanations below it. This will help you to know Him in a practical way through your experiences.

Extract from Sakar Murli of 21-7-20 / 21-7-20:

'Who is explaining this? The spiritual Father. ...He has been given many names. There is also a great deal of praise of the Father. This is the praise of the Supreme Father, the Supreme Soul, is it not? ...He is very beautiful because He is ever pure. ... The beautiful Supreme Father, the Supreme Soul, to whom people have been calling out "O Shiv Baba!" on the path of devotion, that incorporeal Supreme Father, the Supreme Soul, has now come to change impure souls into pure souls and make them beautiful. ...The Father is also called the Flame, but He is, in fact, the Supreme Soul. Just as each of you is called a soul, so He is also called the Supreme Soul. ...The Father, who is the Ocean of Knowledge and the Ocean of Purity, Himself, says: I don't take rebirth. ...The Supreme Father, the Supreme Soul, comes here to meet you children. He meets you through this body. ...You eat and drink with the unlimited Father. ...You remember the Father. You say: You are the Mother and Father. A child continues to play with his father. ...All souls are the children of the Supreme Father, the Supreme Soul. ...You have found the Satguru, the Father, who takes you back. ...Only the one Father is the Purifier. Therefore, when He comes, souls surely have to be made pure. ...The Father comes to make you beautiful from ugly. The Father says: I am also your true, obedient Father. A father is always obedient to his children. He serves them so much! ...The parlokik Father also says: I have come to purify you.' (**Sakar Murli 21-7-20**)

Explanations on the murli extract for churning:

God is an incorporeal, pure Point of living Light who resides in the Soul World which is way beyond the Corporeal World. God does not take births in the Corporeal World like how human souls do.

There is only one God and it is this same God that has been worshipped by human beings through various different names. God, the Supreme Soul, is the Father of all human souls.

From the Copper Age, we (the souls) have been calling Him to come and purify us again, and He has now come to transform us from the impure state to the pure brilliantly beautiful state. He came and used the body of Brahma Baba to give us this knowledge so as to transform us into the pure divine state. God teaches us as our Father, Mother and Satguru so that we become spiritually powerful before He takes us back Home to the Soul World.

God is our spiritual Father, parlokik Father or Supreme Father. However, since we have all relationships with Him, He is also our Mother. As our Father and Mother, He takes care of us and provides us with whatever we want or need. As God's children, we have to develop a close relationship with Him now so that we can easily remain in yoga with Him. Through our yoga, we become like Baba, i.e. we would be brilliantly radiating out His vibrations into the world.

When Shiv Baba began using the corporeal body of Brahma Baba, BKs were eating and drinking with Him. However, now, we have to be trained to eat and drink while in yoga with God because this makes us spiritually powerful. It is through spiritual effort making that our spiritual strength increases with time. We have to develop our relationship with Baba through eating and drinking while in remembrance. For example, we have to visualize that Baba is giving powerful vibrations to the food which we eat so that we can become spiritually powerful. We should be happy that Baba is giving us His attention so that we become spiritually powerful.

The Sanskrit meaning of Satguru or Sadguru is "the true guru". God is the true Satguru since only God can guide us on the true spiritual path so that we attain self-realisation. Through self-realisation we become aware that we are actually the soul and not the body. Only God can enable us to experience ourselves as the soul. It is God who is the Supreme Lord of Truth since Truth (sat) can only be taught by the Supreme Guru (God). Since He is an Ocean of Knowledge and an Ocean of Purity, He teaches us and purifies us so that He can take us back to the Soul World. Only God, the Purifier, can take everyone back Home because all souls have to be purified before they are taken back.

Keep seeing God as your Satguru so that you can be properly taught the Truth while you are on this spiritual path. If your spiritual stage was good while you read or listen to the knowledge given by Him, God will be subtly teaching you (the soul) too.

Chapter 4: Using the Mind, Intellect and Sanskaras to Churn and to do Service

In the murli extract, which can be found further down, Baba asks us to use the intellect to do service. Through doing service now, we accumulate spiritual income. This **spiritual income** gives us:

1. spiritual strength now so that we enjoy greater stability, happiness, bliss and peace.

2. more benefits in the Golden and Silver Ages.

You should keep accumulating spiritual income so that you can enjoy the above benefits to a greater and greater extent. Actually, you can also use your spiritual income in this birth itself through enjoying name, fame etc. However, if you did this, your enjoyment will be less in the Golden and Silver Ages. It will be better to enjoy God's Company now than to use your spiritual income in this birth itself. Through keeping God's Company, you will have inner stability and live a blissful life.

It should be noted that you will accumulate a huge spiritual income for all the benefits which others enjoy due to the service which you do. Therefore, give the BK knowledge to others so that they can also churn the knowledge to enjoy all the benefits. Through doing this service, you are helping others to experience peace and happiness.

Though it is good to do service, make sure that you have become spiritually powerful and have understood the BK knowledge properly before explaining the knowledge to others. When you are doing service, also make sure that you are in a high spiritual stage, through having churned the knowledge, so that God can use you to explain the knowledge to them (via your link to Him). When your spiritual stage is high, He will put the knowledge in your mind (through your link to Him) so that you can explain what is in your mind to others.

If you have not been in BK Gyan for many years (to become spiritually powerful and have a better understanding on the knowledge), you can easily do service through:

1. providing the BK materials for others to read.

2. introducing others to good BK teachers.

In order to have a better understanding on the knowledge, you should use the mind, intellect and sanskaras efficiently. The mind, intellect and memory bank (sanskaras) are the three functions of the soul. You create thoughts in your mind. Further, all the information, which is perceived through the five senses, comes into the mind. Therefore, what you see, read, hear etc come into your mind for you (the soul) to perceive. The intellect brings all the information, which is in the mind, to the memory bank so that they can be stored there. Further, while we read, see etc, the intellect brings information from the memory bank to the mind so that we can:

1. understand what we are reading, etc.

2. know what we are seeing etc.

The soul also uses the intellect to understand, judge, discriminate, reason, assess, etc.

You can easily keep your intellect connected in yoga with God when you use the mind, intellect and sanskaras efficiently. You can use your mind, intellect and sanskaras efficiently when:

1. your mind, intellect and memory bank are filled with the BK knowledge.

2. you (the soul) have become spiritually powerful through making spiritual efforts over a long period of time.

3. you are in a spiritually powerful stage due to being in yoga with God.

Since you use your mind, intellect and sanskaras efficiently, you can easily continue keeping your intellect connected in yoga with God.

When you use your mind to create thoughts that are based on the BK knowledge, there is knowledge in your mind. When the intellect is used to understand the knowledge which is in the mind:

1. the intellect also gets filled with the knowledge that is in the mind.

2. your intellect becomes divine since it gets exposed to God's Sounds of Silence that accompany the knowledge.

3. your divine intellect flies to get you linked to God.

When your mind and intellect are filled with the knowledge, there is no place for 'bad thoughts and emotions' in your mind. The vices cannot come into your mind so as to influence you because you are filled with this powerful knowledge that keeps you linked to God. So you easily remain linked to God.

When you have established your link to God/Baba through using your intellect to churn the knowledge:

1. God's powerful Virtues and Powers will flow into you (the soul) through your link to Him since God is an 'Ocean of Divine Virtues and Powers'.

2. you will be able to understand the BK knowledge more clearly through your link since God is the Ocean of Knowledge.

There are also numerous other benefits enjoyed if you keep making spiritual efforts through churning the knowledge.

When you no longer focus on a point of knowledge, which is in your mind, the intellect takes that from the mind and puts it in the memory bank. The experiences, which you enjoy through having attained a powerful stage, are also taken to the memory bank (from the mind) by the intellect. Through all these, your memory bank gets filled with knowledge and 'memories of powerful experiences'. When you want to recollect the knowledge, experiences, etc, the intellect brings the knowledge, experiences etc from the memory bank to your mind. If the memory bank is filled with knowledge and experiences, the intellect will easily bring these into your mind (from the memory bank). As a consequence, you can easily remain in yoga with God.

After the following murli extract, there are more explanations on how the mind, intellect and sanskaras are used. Keep rereading the following murli extract and the explanations below it because this will:

1. keep filling your mind, intellect and memory bank with God's knowledge, and

2. keep your intellect connected in yoga with God.

"The main *points* should be written down in a book so *clearly* that anyone who reads it will automatically understand this knowledge. Because these are the versions spoken by God Shiva, they will enjoy reading them. This is something for intellects to do."

(Sakar Murli 14-8-20)

Explanations on the murli extract for churning:

If non-BKs read the murli, they will not understand half of what is being explained in it. Thus, we have to churn the knowledge in the murli and then explain the murli points clearly so that others can understand it. Since we are explaining Baba's knowledge and Baba is using us as instruments to explain the knowledge, Baba's Sounds of Silence will also accompany the words which we use to explain the knowledge. Hence, the reader's experiences would be good and they will enjoy reading it. If those reading the explanations were deity souls, the souls will be touched by Baba's Light to bring them into the Brahma Kumaris. Hence, they will have a very good experience as they read the explanations on the murli points. They will surely want to receive more of the BK knowledge.

When we contemplate on the knowledge, we are actually churning the knowledge because we keep thinking about the knowledge from various aspects through using our mind, intellect and memory bank which are the three faculties of the soul. Even the person who reads our explanations is using the mind, intellect and memory bank.

When a person reads the explanations on the murli points, what is being read is brought into the mind (through the eyes). Thus, the soul reads what has been brought into the mind, as the person reads the book. When the words are in the mind, the intellect brings information from the memory bank so that the soul can read what has been brought into the mind. All that which we learnt, while we were learning to read in school etc, will be brought into the mind so that we can read the words. If the explanation is in another language, which we have not learnt, there will not be any relevant information in the memory bank which the intellect can bring to enable us to read it.

When a person reads the explanations in the language known to him/her, the intellect is also used to assess and understand what is being read. The more we try to understand it, the more we use the intellect. If we were reading it while we were in the ordinary state, the intellect will just bring whatever is in the memory bank so as to enable us to have a better understanding. However, if we were reading the explanations with faith that it is from God, the intellect gets exposed to the Sounds of Silence that accompany the words; thus, the intellect becomes divine and flies to link the soul to Baba. Hence, the soul:

1. also gets knowledge/information from the Ocean of Knowledge (God/Baba) to understand what is being read, and

2. has a good experience (since the soul is exposed to Baba's pure Virtues and Powers).

To make sure that a soul, who is new to Gyan, understands what is being read, we have to churn the knowledge through using our intellect, before explaining it to them. If one does not have faith in the knowledge, one is just reading the knowledge and not churning the knowledge. When we churn the knowledge, jewels of knowledge and other valuables emerge from the Ocean (Baba/God) for our benefit. We are exposed to Baba's pure Virtues and Powers. At the same time, Baba assists us by giving us the relevant knowledge which gives us a better understanding.

We have to make sure that we are linked to the Ocean of Knowledge so that we get valuable knowledge. Through using the additional knowledge, which we receive from Baba, we will be able to give a very good explanation to the readers so that they have a better understanding.

While contemplating on the knowledge, we should not indulge in the vices. This keeps the intellect in a pure and clean state (without the intellect being tainted by the impure vices) so that we get a clear understanding, on the knowledge, through our yoga with Baba. Our explanations would be good and easy to understand, if we maintained our pure state.

Baba does not give all the explanations in the murlis because we are encouraged to make spiritual efforts to understand the knowledge. Through making spiritual efforts, we become spiritually powerful and so the Golden Aged world gets created, i.e. our goals are achieved.

Chapter 5: Soul, God and their Three Faculties

The essence of all the knowledge in the murlis is to:

1. see yourself as the soul, and

2. see God as the Supreme Soul.

God gives us knowledge about the soul and Supreme Soul in different ways so as to instil this knowledge into us. For example, in the following murli extract, He explains how the soul and Supreme Soul cannot be decorated, and that it is only the physical body which is decorated.

In order to remain linked to God through remaining stable in the form of the soul, we have to:

1. keep seeing ourselves as the soul who is in the body, and

2. keep contemplating on the various aspects of the soul and Supreme Soul.

When you think about the mind, intellect and sanskaras of the soul and Supreme Soul, you are also thinking about the various aspects of the soul and Supreme Soul. Therefore, further down, the explanations also touch on the knowledge that both (the soul and Supreme Soul) have a mind, intellect and memory bank.

Extract from Sakar Murli dated 14-7-20:

"However, the mind and intellect are organs of the soul. ...A soul is called a soul. In the same way, He is the Supreme Soul. He says: I am the Supreme Soul, that is, I am God, your Father. ...Just as souls cannot be decorated, in the same way, the Supreme Soul cannot be decorated; He is just a point. All the decoration is only of the body. The Father says:

39

Neither am I decorated nor are souls decorated. Souls are just points. Such a tiny point cannot play a part. When a tiny soul enters a body, the body is decorated in so many different ways."

(Sakar Murli 14-7-20)

Explanations on the murli extract for churning:

You (the soul) are a metaphysical point of living white light. The mind, intellect and sanskaras (memory bank) are your ministers, faculties or organs. We (the souls) cannot play our parts in the World Drama, on earth, without a body. So you (the soul) enter a body to play your part on earth. It is the body which gets decorated in the Corporeal World.

God is also a metaphysical Point of living white light. God is the Supreme Soul and He is the Father of all souls. Where spiritual strength is concerned, God is like an Ocean while we are like a drop in comparison. God does not take births, like us, on earth.

God also has a Mind, Intellect and Sanskaras (Memory Bank). During the Confluence Age, our mind, intellect and sanskaras connect to God's Mind, Intellect and Sanskaras when we are in yoga with God. So God is able to guide us, as we become spiritually powerful.

Chapter 6: Third Eye of Knowledge

"Just as these organs are of the body, so, the mind, the intellect and this eye too are organs of souls. This eye is not like physical eyes. ...Each of you souls receives a third eye of knowledge. It is the Father who gives it."

(Sakar Murli 14-7-20)

Explanations on the murli extract for churning:

The eye referred to in the above murli extract is the third eye.

During the Confluence Age, Baba opens our third eye by giving us the knowledge in the murlis. As you (the soul) receive this knowledge, you receive the third eye of knowledge. To receive this third eye of knowledge one has to accept the knowledge so as to be exposed to God's vibrations which accompany the knowledge. Through this our intellect, which was in the ordinary state, becomes the divine intellect. Since the divine intellect is the subtle eye of the soul, our third eye gets opened. The mind is used by the soul to think, see what has come into the mind, etc. The intellect and divine intellect is used by the soul to contemplate, decide, judge, etc. However, when the divine intellect is used to link itself to God and to communicate with God, the divine intellect is used as the subtle eye of the soul for this purpose. Since the mind is used to see the visions, etc which we perceive through using the divine intellect, it can be said that the mind also plays a role together with the 'divine intellect and knowledge' as the third eye. However, to be more specific, it is the knowledge, which is within the soul, that is the third eye because it enables the soul to get linked to God, etc. When our third eye is opened, we are in God's Company and we are being guided by God. We will understand the knowledge through God's guidance.

When the third eye of the soul is opened, the pineal gland, which is in the brain, also becomes active; so we can subtly see God, visions etc. Non- BKs says that the pineal gland is the third eye because they use it to have subtle experiences etc. However, where BKs are concerned, the third eye is the BK knowledge and our divine intellect because these, together, enable us to have a subtle relationship with God. To be more accurate, it can be said that it is the knowledge, which is within the soul, that is the third eye because it is the knowledge which helps us to have a subtle relationship with God. Thus, use the knowledge so that you get God's guidance and help. Keep your third eye open through constantly contemplating on the BK knowledge.

Chapter 7: Churn the Ocean of Knowledge

We are churning the ocean of knowledge when we churn the knowledge in our mind because:

1. our mind, intellect and sanskaras are connected to God's Mind, Intellect and Sanskaras when we are linked to God. Since there is a link, the knowledge which is in our mind is linked to the ocean of knowledge which is within God. Due to the link and the churning, **new points of knowledge** will flow into our mind from the Ocean of Knowledge (God).

2. God's powerful Sounds of Silence accompany the knowledge which He has given. Through these Sounds of Silence, the knowledge which is in our mind is connected to the ocean of knowledge which is within God. The more our mind is filled with knowledge (for churning purposes), the greater the connection to the ocean of knowledge which is within God.

The knowledge (which is in your mind, intellect and sanskaras) links you:

1. to the Ocean of Knowledge (God), and

2. to the ocean of knowledge (the knowledge) which is within the Ocean of Knowledge (God).

Since the knowledge which you are churning on is connected to all the knowledge that within God, you are churning an ocean of knowledge. However, in order to churn the ocean of knowledge, you must deeply contemplate on the knowledge until you attain a high stage. If you have attained the high stage, then, you are churning the ocean of knowledge. When you are in a spiritually high stage, you will be able to churn the ocean of knowledge more efficiently to have an even better understanding on the knowledge; you will have a better understanding because new points of knowledge emerge from the ocean of knowledge when your stage is high.

God is the Ocean of Knowledge. However, He has only given knowledge in a nutshell to mankind for world transformation through self-transformation. We have to keep churning the knowledge so that new points of knowledge keep emerging from the ocean of knowledge.

It should be remembered that we are students. This means that we must keep churning so that our understanding keeps improving. Our faith also increases as we keep having a better understanding on the knowledge. The stronger our faith, the easier it will be to churn the ocean of knowledge in order to have an even better understanding on the knowledge.

You will understand the following murli extract based on the above explanations. More explanations, on churning the knowledge, can be found after the following murli extract.

Murli Extract:

"You children have to churn the ocean of knowledge; only then will *points* emerge."

(Sakar Murli 11-8-20)

Explanations on the murli extract for churning:

Churning the knowledge, or murli point, involves thinking deeply about it. You have to keep contemplating on the knowledge intensely, from various angles, with faith that it is the Truth. While churning, you use your intellect to turn the knowledge around:

1. within your mind, and

2. between your mind and Memory Bank. Knowledge, which was previously contemplated on, and previous experiences are emerged by the intellect (from the Memory Bank) so that you can have a better

understanding on the new murli point that you are now contemplating on.

If your spiritual stage was not good, you understand the murli points based on the gross meaning of the words used. When you do this, you will only understand about half of what Baba is teaching. You have to understand the remainder half through churning the knowledge. When you churn on a murli point, you get linked to Baba; thus, you receive more knowledge through your yoga with Baba. The knowledge, which you receive through your yoga with Baba, emerges from the Ocean of Knowledge (God/Baba). What you receive through this way will give you a good understanding on the murli point. You have actually churned the knowledge to extract the deeper meaning which the murli point has. When you understand a murli point, you can accept the murli point to be the Truth. It will make a lot of sense to you though it does not make much sense to someone who is new to Gyan. You have to keep churning the knowledge so that your understanding improves, with time. Sometimes, it might take a few years to:

1. understand a murli point. When you become spiritually power, you can easily attain a stage where your churning enables you to understand the murli point.

2. enjoy the ability to instantly understand knowledge through the churning process. This ability improves as you become spiritually powerful.

When you churn the knowledge, you have to think deeply on the knowledge so as to understand it and to enjoy the blissful stage. Since you become spiritually powerful, as you churn, you will attain the pure blissful stage while you churn the murli point. These benefits are part of the 'butter' which is received through the churning of the milk/knowledge. These are like butter because they are very valuable. You have to keep contemplating on the knowledge until you get saturated with the knowledge so that you get the benefits of the churning process.

Chapter 8: Milk of Knowledge

There are two murli extracts below on the milk of knowledge. Further explanations are given after these two murli extracts so that you can have a better understanding on the milk of knowledge.

1. "The Father sits here and tells you the meaning through this mouth and so this is the Gaumukh.... Shiv Baba says: I give you the milk of knowledge through this mouth and so all your sins are burnt away and you souls become pure. So, you then receive pure bodies."

(Sakar Murli 4-9-2019)

2. "The Father gives you the milk of knowledge to drink..."

(Sakar Murli 14-11-2018)

Explanations on the murli extract for churning:

This knowledge has been referred to as the milk of knowledge in the murlis because:

1. Baba is nourishing us (His children) through this knowledge, like how milk nourishes babies etc.

2. this knowledge is very valuable like milk. It is valuable since it is the means through which we get linked to God. We will not be able to link ourselves to God and get nourished, if we did not have this knowledge.

During the Confluence Age, we are nourished when we contemplate on the knowledge, which God has given in the murlis, because when we contemplate on the knowledge:

1. the intellect is **empowered** to 'become divine and link us to God', and

2. God's pure light flows into us (the souls) so as to empower us.

When one churns with faith and acceptance, one's intellect is able to absorb God's Sounds of Silence which accompany the knowledge. Through the Sounds of Silence, the intellect also absorbs God's Power of Silence. As a consequence, the intellect is nourished by God's powerful vibrations which are like milk that nourishes the intellect and enables it to:

1. fly to the Subtle Region, and

2. link the soul to God who is in the Subtle Region during the Confluence Age.

When the soul is linked to God, God's powerful vibrations flow into the soul to continue nourishing the soul in a powerful way; it is as if one is drinking Baba's vibrations, as one gets energised, when God's Milky Light flows into the soul.

Since God's Sounds of Silence accompany the knowledge which we are churning:

1. it is like we are churning milk when we churn the knowledge.

2. we are getting God's assistance to establish a powerful link to Him.

3. the knowledge is milk that enables the intellect to get nourished so as to transform into the divine state. Since the intellect becomes the divine intellect, it has the ability to link the soul to God. Then, since we are linked to God, God's powerful vibrations continuously flow into the soul for transforming the soul into the divine state. As the light of the soul transforms into the pure divine state, the soul becomes more and more spiritually powerful. The soul continues to be nourished through the link to God, when we continue to churn the knowledge.

When you churn the knowledge intensely, you (the soul) **absorb the knowledge**, i.e. you are **drinking the milk/knowledge**. As you drink the knowledge/milk, you are also absorbing/drinking Baba's vibrations. So you are being nourished to become spiritually powerful and divine. The more you churn the knowledge, the more you are drinking the knowledge. At the same time, you are absorbing more nourishment because:

1. the knowledge is accompanied by Baba's vibrations.

2. more of God's Light flows into you to empower you.

When there is more knowledge within you, there is more of Baba's Sounds of Silence within you. Thus, your intellect is energised to a greater extent, and it will establish a stronger link to God. When there is a stronger link, you absorb/drink more of Baba's Light to nourish yourself.

The knowledge which God has given us is also within Him. When you are **linked to God**, the knowledge (which is within you) connects to the knowledge which is within God as your sanskaras (memory bank) connects to God's Sanskaras (Memory Bank). As a result, you enjoy greater nourishment.

Since the knowledge and the Sounds of Silence are from God; they can be seen as being part and parcel of God. Therefore, they help us to establish a strong link to God. God assists us, initially, through this way. God's assistance, during the churning process, is part and parcel of the 'milk' that helps to nourish us. Since God has enabled us to get linked to Him through the churning process, we only have to churn the knowledge so as to grab God's Helping Hand to get nourished further.

Milk enables babies to grow in a healthy manner. Similarly, churning the knowledge provides nourishment (to enable us to grow) so that we:

1. become spiritually powerful.

2. transform into deities and have the ability to live in the Golden Aged world.

As we become spiritually powerful, through churning the knowledge:

1. it is as if our Golden Aged deity self (Krishna) is growing.

2. our ability to become Vishnu (in the Golden Age) grows.

During the Confluence Age, as we (the souls) transform into the divine state, Krishna/Vishnu is also growing (getting created). Therefore, when the Golden Aged world materialises:

1. we take our next birth as Krishna, and

2. we become Vishnu, when we get married during our births in the Golden Age.

During the Confluence Age, God's Light and the Subtle Region act like the womb within which we grow. Due to drinking the milk of knowledge, we can also have an experience of being in the ocean of milk (Golden Age) while we are in Vishnupuri. Vishnupuri is in the middle section of the Subtle Region, which exists during the Confluence Age. Vishnupuri is also filled with God's Light since it is in the Subtle Region. It is like we are in the ocean of milk when we are in Vishnupuri because:

1. God is sustaining us, now. So He enables us to enjoy **Golden Aged experiences.**

2. God's powerful, pure, divine vibrations surround us to **transform** us into the divine state. We are bathing in His pure energising divine Milky Light, as we experience our transformed divine state.

God does not take a birth in the Golden Age to sustain the Golden Aged world; it is we who take births in the Golden Age and sustain the world to remain in the divine state. Since God has transformed us into the pure divine state, we are able to sustain the Golden Aged world in its divine state, after God creates the Golden Aged world through using us. Now, while we are in the Subtle Region that is filled with God's divine light, we subtly grow to become the divine deities:

1. who will live in the materialised heavenly world which exists in the Golden Age (ocean of milk).

2. who will have the ability to maintain the world in its divine state, during the Golden Age.

When we keep churning the knowledge, God's blissful milky vibrations keep flowing into us for our spiritual growth; hence, we can attain even higher spiritually powerful stages, as time progresses. By the end of the Confluence Age, many of us will be in a very powerful stage. At that time, God's powerful presence will be experienced by many, through the powerful gathering, because:

1. many BKs will be closely linked to God.

2. God is an Ocean.

Since God's vibrations vibrate out from us to fill the world and Subtle Region, other weaker souls will be in a powerful environment. The Power of the Gathering will help them to easily:

1. attain a pure powerful stage, and

2. remain as BKs.

The world will also transform into the Golden Aged world in a material way due to the Power of the Gathering. The 'milk' also represents the nourishment which the 'souls and world' receive through the Power of the Gathering. Through this nourishment, many will be helped to enjoy bliss, stability and a heavenly life.

Since Baba is nourishing us through this knowledge, now:

1. we (the souls) become pure and spiritually powerful, as we get filled with divine virtues and powers.

2. we transform into the divine Golden Aged state. As we transform, our world also transforms. Only the nourishment that is from God can transform us and our world.

3. all deity souls will be able to live their lives, during the first half cycle. Though all deity souls will receive this knowledge, many of them will not be powerful spiritual effort makers. They will be sustained by the Power of the Gathering, at the end of the Cycle. Then, when the world transforms into the Golden Aged world, through the Power of the Gathering, they will take their next birth in the first half cycle.

One takes a new spiritual birth when one receives the BK knowledge. This spiritual life is then sustained through the churning process, i.e. we will grow to become spiritually powerful as we churn the knowledge. The more we grow spiritually now, the longer we (the deity souls) live in the first half cycle. The longer we live in the first half cycle, the earlier we take our first birth there, e.g. we might take our first at the beginning of the Golden Age. This also means that we would be able to take more births as deities in the first half cycle. We will be able to enjoy to a greater extent in the heavenly world, if we take more births there. We should take as much nourishment as possible from Baba, now, so that we can take the first birth at the beginning of the Golden Age because the 'loveliest world to live in' will exist at the beginning of the Golden Age.

When we churn, God also gives us experiences so that we understand the knowledge, etc. Our stage is high when we have these experiences. Thus, when we recollect these experiences, we instantly go beyond to attain a high spiritual stage again; consequently, we continue to grow spiritually. All these experiences are also part of the nourishment which we receive due to the churning process. We can live a blissful life now, through constantly having experiences, if we churn the knowledge/milk. Further, since we are becoming virtuous and spiritually powerful:

1. we will find it easier to remain peaceful and happy, and

2. our stability improves.

Due to the above, we will find it easy to remain happy while we carry out our daily activities. We enjoy benefits now, while we also enjoy the benefit of being able to take our next birth in the Golden Aged world. Due to receiving nourishment from God now, we will receive pure bodies which cannot get diseased at all, during our lives in the first half cycle.

Since the knowledge and God's Light enable the soul to transform into the divine state, these are the nutritious milk through which butter is extracted. This butter represents all the benefits which you receive through the churning process. When you churn the knowledge with faith, you will be extracting the butter from the milk because you will be receiving all the numerous benefits which are acquired through churning the knowledge. You should have firm faith in the knowledge so that you (the soul) and your intellect become the golden vessel which contains the milk/knowledge as you churn the knowledge. You and your intellect will be golden because you (the soul) will be in the pure, divine state when you churn the knowledge.

In the above first murli extract, God says that Brahma Baba's mouth is Gaumukh because God (Shiv Baba) enters the body of Brahma Baba to give the knowledge (milk of knowledge) through Brahma Baba's mouth, during the Confluence Age.

Gau means cow and mukh means mouth. Therefore, Gaumukh means "the cow's mouth". Brahma Baba's mouth is viewed as the cow's mouth because:

1. the knowledge, which is given through Brahma Baba's mouth, is the milk of knowledge.

2. nourishing milk is received through the body of the cow.

3. the significance of Gaumukh is explained by Baba, from the Confluence Aged point of view.

After the deity souls lost their divine world, at the end of the Silver Age, they had created the figure of the Gaumukh as a memorial of how God's knowledge flows out through Brahma Baba's mouth during the Confluence Age. They created the image of the Gaumukh because memories, of what had happened during the previous Confluence Age, emerged to influence the deity souls from the end of the Silver Age. As these memories emerged, the deity souls knew that they were able to live in the heavenly world (which they were losing) because they were purified, through receiving the knowledge that had flowed out from the Gaumukh, during the previous Confluence Age. From the beginning of the Copper Age, these deity souls were waiting for the day when they will be purified again (as they were during the previous Confluence Age) because:

1. the Confluence Aged memories continued to emerge to influence them.

2. the deity souls had already lost their divine world.

3. they wanted to live in their Golden Aged world again.

These deity souls desired to be purified again though, as the person, they may not have been aware of this inner deep desire. They continued to give a lot of importance to the Gaumukh because:

1. memories continued to emerge on how the milk of knowledge, which was received through the mouth of Brahma Baba, purified them.

2. their ancestors, who walked out of the Silver Age, had given importance to the Gaumukh.

3. the Gaumukh began to be seen as the source of the waters which flow in the River Ganga.

Hindus belief that the waters of the River Ganga purifies those who bath in it. This belief was created, during ancient times, based on the memories that emerged in respect of how the knowledge, which we gave (as Ganga) during the Confluence Age, enabled all those who bathed in the knowledge to get purified. When our stage is high, God Shiva uses us (through our link to Him) to give knowledge to others. When He does this, we are playing the role of Ganga because we are used to give the knowledge. The souls, who intensely contemplate on this knowledge, are bathing in the knowledge because they (the souls) are completely filled with knowledge. As they bath in the knowledge, God's Light washes off all their impurities through the purification process.

The soul is purified when it is filled with knowledge because:

1. the soul gets linked to God when we churn the knowledge, and

2. God's light purifies the soul when we are linked to God.

During the purification process, since we are exposed to God's powerful Light:

1. all our sins are burnt away and we (the souls) become pure. As the sins are burnt away, we become purer; hence we become spiritually more powerful.

2. our impure light energies are transformed into pure divine light energies. Therefore, we become purer, spiritually more powerful and divine.

As you keep churning the knowledge (milk), you keep getting purified while you are also nourished. Then, you will be able to take births in the ocean of milk (Golden Age) where you enjoy the pure state through using pure bodies. Keep churning this knowledge in order to enjoy all the numerous benefits. You are churning the nourishing milk of knowledge when you churn the knowledge.

Chapter 9: Cycle of 84 Births

When you churn on how you (the soul) have taken 84 births through the Cycle of Time, you should believe:

1. that you are a soul (a point of light), and

2. that Time flows in a cyclic manner.

As you keep churning on what happens, as you take your 84 births during each Cycle, you can easily experience yourself as the blissful soul because you are contemplating on the knowledge which has been given by God Himself. So keep contemplating on what has been said in the following murli extract and in the explanations below that.

"You children know the cycle of 84 births. You now have to return home. Therefore, you also have to remember the Father so that your sins can be cut away."

(Sakar Murli 13-7-20)

Explanations on the murli extract for churning:

The Cycle of Time is about how time flows in a cyclic manner through the following Ages:

1. Golden Age or Satyuga. In this Age we take 8 births.

2. Silver Age or Tretayuga. In this Age we take 12 births.

3. Copper Age or Dwapuryuga. In this Age we take 21 births.

4. Iron Age or Kaliyuga. In this Age we take 42 births.

5. Confluence Age or Sangamyuga (The Confluence between Kaliyug and the Golden Age). In this Age we take 1 birth.

Keep remembering that we take a total of 84 births in each cycle, as explained above. At the end of each cycle, during the Confluence Age, we get purified before God takes us back to the Soul World. We have to keep remembering Baba so that our sins are burnt away while we are in the Confluence Age. If not, when we leave the body, we might experience punishment while we are on our way back to the Soul World with God. Therefore, keep remembering that you are going to take your next birth in the heavenly Golden Aged world so that you get purified while enjoying bliss now. You become spiritually powerful through this and you will enjoy a lot of benefits in this life itself, for example, you will find it easier and easier to remain happy and peaceful when you become more and more pure.

Chapter 10: Churning on the World Ladder

From the beginning of the Golden Age, as the embodied souls were living their lives in the Corporeal World, they were losing their spiritual strength. They were getting spiritually weaker and weaker as they were taking the 83 births in the Cycle. In the picture of the World Ladder, this has been portrayed through the embodied souls walking down the World Ladder. Now, as you churn on the BK knowledge, you are taking a high jump to the top of the World Ladder. Therefore, be happy that you are flying up to the top of the World Ladder now, while you contemplate on how you had climbed down the World Ladder from the beginning of the last Golden Age until you came into the Confluence Age. The World Ladder is explained after the following murli extract.

Extract from Sakar Murli of 20-7-20:

"At present, everyone is a resident of hell. The Father now says that you were full of all virtues. You have now become so tamopradhan! You have continued to come down the ladder. ... You know that you became impure while taking 84 births and that that was why you called out to the Purifier Father. When you use pictures to explain, it becomes easy for people to understand. The full 84 births are explained in detail in the picture of the ladder."

(Sakar Murli 20-7-20)

Explanations on the murli extract for churning:

As I explain about the World Ladder, further below, remember that it is God who gave this knowledge. Do not wonder if it is true or not.

Just accept it, while reading it, and then keep thinking about it so that you will have a good spiritual understanding on it. Baba will give you a good understanding on it if you keep a good spiritual stage as you read it. Do not feel miserable that Mankind is walking down the ladder. Feel happy that you are being given an understanding on why you have come into a bad state, which is why Baba has come to uplift you into the divine Golden Aged state again. Think of how fortunate you are that you can take a high jump to the very top of the World Ladder in just one birth, now, whereas Mankind took so long to come down the World Ladder.

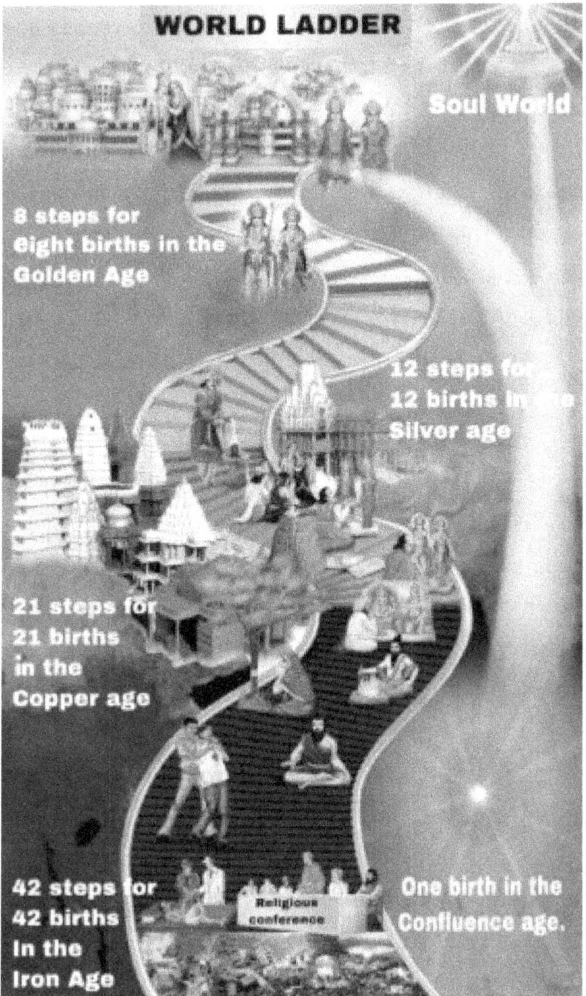

The World Ladder or Ladder of 84 births is used to explain the rise and fall of Mankind. It is used to explain how human beings walk down the World Ladder as the spiritual strength of the souls decrease. Each step, in the World Ladder, represents a birth. The deities of the Golden Age walk down from the beginning of the Golden Aged section of the Ladder. The 8 steps in the Golden Aged section of the World Ladder represents that Lakshmi and Narayan, the rulers in the Golden Aged world, take 8 births in the Golden Age. They are on the highest step in the World Ladder, during their first birth. Then, they are on the step below that, during their second birth. This portrays that the soul has lost some spiritual strength and is walking down the World Ladder, as a result. They will be on the third step during their third birth because they continue losing spiritual strength. They continue walking down during each birth until they are on the eighth step at the end of the Golden Age.

There are 12 steps, in the Silver Aged section of the World Ladder. This reflects that Rama and Sita, the rulers in the Silver Aged world, take 12 births in the Silver Age. They continue walking down the Ladder since they continue losing spiritual strength. Thus, by the end of the Silver Age, they reach the end of the Silver Aged section of the World Ladder. The deities are divine until the end of the Silver Age.

Then, at the beginning of the Copper Age, which begins the Copper Aged section of the Ladder, they transform into the ordinary state. The people lose their divine state, and they become more and more impure as they walk down the Ladder.

The 21 steps in the Copper Aged section of the World Ladder represents that souls take 21 births in the Copper Age. Since their spiritual strength continues to decrease, they continue walking down the World Ladder as they take subsequent births. During their last birth, in the Copper Age, they will be on the last step, at the end of the Copper Aged section of the World Ladder.

In the Iron Aged section of the World Ladder, there are 42 steps representing that the soul takes 42 births in Kaliyug. Since the soul keeps losing spiritual strength, the person keeps stepping down on the World Ladder until the soul is at the end of the World Ladder. The soul is in the most impure state (tamopradhan state) by the end of Kaliyug. It is hell on earth because everyone is indulging in the vices to a great extent. Though the human beings are not aware of it, the souls will be calling out to God to 'come and purify the soul' so that the souls can live a heavenly life.

God comes, around the end of Kaliyug, and begins the Confluence Age. During the Confluence Age, through just one spiritual birth, the soul gets recharged and gets transformed into the Golden Aged state again. The soul flies to the top of the Ladder again. The transformed soul goes back to the Soul World so as to take its next birth on the first step, at the top of the World Ladder.

The explanations on the World Ladder reflect what happens during each Cycle of Time. Since we only take one spiritual birth in the Confluence Age, we can take a maximum of 84 births in a cycle. How fortunate we are that we only take 84 births in a Cycle and not numerous more births.

Chapter 11: Nectar of Knowledge and Remembrance

The knowledge, which has been given by God in the murlis, is referred to as gyān amrit (nectar of knowledge) because we experience the sweetness of nectar when we churn the knowledge. This sweetness is experienced because:

1. the soul is filled with knowledge that is accompanied by God's Sounds of Silence.

2. the intellect is empowered by God's Sounds of Silence (which accompany the knowledge) to become the divine intellect.

3. the divine intellect instantly flies to link the soul to God.

4. God's sweet Divine Virtues and Powers flow into the soul through the link between the soul and God.

5. we enjoy the sweet satoguni (pure) stage, now, during the Confluence Age.

6. the soul is slowly transforming into the sweet, divine Golden Aged satopradhan state. We are only in the pure, divine satopradhan state during our births in the ocean of milk (Golden Age). However, now, we can taste the sweetness of the divine state, during experiences, since God is transforming us into the divine state.

It should be noted that God's Sounds of Silence, which accompany the knowledge, are connected to God because:

1. they are connected to God's Power of Silence.

2. they are connected to the knowledge within God.

3. they are vibrations from God.

When we are linked to God, we will surely experience the knowledge as the nectar of knowledge. For the reason that the knowledge is meant to link us to God, **it is** nectar of knowledge. Acceptance that this knowledge is from God, instantly links us to God and keeps us linked to God. Thus, we instantly experience the knowledge as nectar of knowledge.

This spiritual knowledge is nectar because:

1. God's vibrations act as the power that enables the soul, who churns the knowledge, to drink the spiritual nectar.

2. God's blessings enable us to get linked to Him when we churn the knowledge.

3. we are remembering God when we remember the knowledge.

God is the Ocean of the Nectar of Knowledge. Only He has the nectar of knowledge; so only He can give us the nectar of knowledge. Remembrance (contemplation on God) is the most important in order to experience the knowledge as the nectar of knowledge. When we remember the knowledge given by God, we are also remembering the One who gave the knowledge to us. We must contemplate on this knowledge because we must remember God. We should keep remembering Baba and the knowledge which He has given, so that we experience the sweetness of nectar.

Since we experience God's blissful vibrations through the 'knowledge and link', it can be said that:

1. we experience the sweetness of nectar when we churn the knowledge.

2. we experience the sweetness of the nectar of knowledge.

The knowledge and remembrance are both nectar that gives life because:

1. the soul becomes spiritually powerful again.

2. we are able to take births in the Golden Age again.

Since Baba has given us the nectar of knowledge and our intellect transforms into the golden divine state when it is filled with the nectar of knowledge, Baba has given us the golden urn which is filled with nectar. This nectar refers to:

1. the golden divine light of the divine intellect, and

2. the nectar of knowledge which the divine intellect is filled with.

We absorb/imbibe/drink the nectar of knowledge as we keep churning this knowledge. This means that we fill our urn (our mind, **divine intellect** and sanskaras) with the nectar of knowledge, as we churn the knowledge. It should be borne in mind that when we churn the knowledge which fills our mind, our intellect is also filled with knowledge because we use the intellect to churn what is in the mind. As a consequence of the churning, the intellect transforms into the divine state. The knowledge, which is in the mind and intellect, is finally used to fill our memory bank with knowledge because whatever is in the mind is taken to the memory bank by the intellect. All these enable us to easily experience the knowledge as the nectar of knowledge because we will be linked to God.

We must keep making spiritual efforts to imbibe the nectar of knowledge since God enables us to drink it now. We can drink the nectar of knowledge at any place and any time. When this nectar of knowledge is in the soul (when we churn on it), it enables us to experience:

1. spiritual intoxication.

2. our true pure, divine state.

We also have to attain a high stage and give the knowledge to others because this enables others to savour the everlasting sweet nectar of spiritual knowledge so as to gain immortality which is received though drinking this nectar. Service should be done while remembering God and the knowledge given by Him because:

1. this also enables us to taste the nectar (the sweetness) of our relationship with God while we do service,

2. God will be using us (through our link to Him) to enable the listener to experience the knowledge as the nectar of knowledge.

More explanations, on the nectar of knowledge, can be found after the following murli extract.

"You are now receiving the nectar of knowledge. However, remembrance is the main thing. It is through this that you become *ever healthy* and *ever wealthy* for 21 births."

(Sakar Murli 30-7-20)

Explanations on the murli extract for churning:

The nectar, which is referred to here, is the sweet nectar of the spiritual knowledge that is given to us by Baba/God in the murlis.

After I was introduced to BK gyan in 1994, I loved hearing BKs explain the knowledge. The impression that was in my mind, when I heard the knowledge, is that it is 'nectar' i.e. something so sweet and lovely. My spiritual stage would be high, when I hear the knowledge, and this may be why I was having this impression in my mind.

The knowledge which Baba gives us is the nectar because:

1. it is so valuable like nectar.

2. the knowledge feels sweet while it in the mind of the soul and while the intellect is churning it.

3. it makes us (the souls) feel sweet.

4. it transforms us into the sweet deities.

5. it enables us to enjoy immortality in the Golden and Silver Ages.

6. it enables us to experience the Truth now.

The above are some of the benefits which we get through drinking or digesting the nectar. We drink or digest the nectar of knowledge by absorbing/imbibing it. We imbibe it through saturating the mind with knowledge and through using the intellect to churn it. Through doing this, the nectar of knowledge will magically transform you into the divine state because you are remembering Baba when you churn the knowledge. Since this knowledge is accompanied by God's Light, we are empowered to digest the nectar. Hence we enjoy the sweet benefits of the nectar.

When you intensely churn this knowledge, you enjoy nectar because the churning of this knowledge emerges the nectar from the Ocean of Knowledge (God), and through drinking or digesting this nectar you will enjoy the benefits. You churn the knowledge through constantly contemplating on it. This churning process can only begin when you have received the knowledge, which has been given by the Ocean of Knowledge, in the murlis.

In the murlis, Baba gives us the knowledge of the soul and Supreme Soul. This is also the nectar of knowledge; so if we keep seeing ourselves as the souls and if we keep remembering Baba, we will be drinking nectar. We transform from ordinary human beings to deities via drinking the nectar of knowledge.

Since the nectar of knowledge is in the soul, we become spiritually intoxicated. The more knowledge there is within us, the greater the intoxication. Thus, keep contemplating on the knowledge which has been given by Baba. This intoxication will enable you to:

1. experience yourself as a Golden Aged deity now

2. become a Golden Aged deity in the next cycle.

Life is meant to be lived with intoxicating happiness. Spiritual intoxication increases our happiness since it increases the spiritual strength of the soul. You have to receive the nectar of knowledge daily so that you constantly remain happy through spiritual intoxication. You receive it through hearing it and reading it.

As we contemplate on the knowledge, we digest the nectar of knowledge. When we do this, we will experience spiritual intoxication. The whole world and you are benefited through this intoxication because Baba's Light will be flowing into the whole world through you (the soul). While you are spiritually intoxicated, you will be eager to do service too, so you will be happy to serve the world.

When your urn is full, you can quench the thirst of all those who are thirsty (for knowledge and spiritual attainment) by giving them the nectar (knowledge) from your urn of knowledge. Through doing this, you earn a huge spiritual income and your spiritual strength increases. As a consequence, you will be able to enjoy nectar (immortality, etc) for a longer time in the Golden Age.

Through giving you the knowledge in the murlis, Baba has given you the 'urn of the nectar of knowledge'. Baba gives us more knowledge when we keep churning the knowledge. So more knowledge gets filled in our urn. Our mind and intellect is also our urn when these are filled with Baba's knowledge. You will understand the knowledge when your mind and intellect are filled with the knowledge (nectar). We should always make sure that our urn is full at all times.

We are so fortunate to have received this knowledge from the Ocean of Knowledge. We will get multimillion-fold benefits through accepting and using this nectar of knowledge for spiritual effort making. To enjoy the nectar, our meditation practices must include contemplation on the knowledge which has been given by Baba. So keep remembering Baba and the knowledge. Through remembering Baba:

1. you will receive perfect bodies which are always healthy during the first half cycle. During the Confluence Age, the soul is ever healthy when one is in the angelic stage. While in the angelic stage, we will be using an angelic body which is not defective in any way. We will not experience pain etc when we use our angelic body.

2. you will also receive wealth for 21 births. During the Confluence Age, we receive wealth which we can use for service. The knowledge itself is also wealth for us because it represents the wealth which we will enjoy in the first half cycle.

Chapter 12: Jewels of Knowledge and Pilgrimage of Remembrance

"Your intellects have remembrance of Shiv Baba alone. Internally you feel that Shiv Baba should say something and give you jewels of knowledge. The Father only comes to give you the jewels of knowledge. He is the Ocean of Knowledge. He says: Children, remain soul conscious. Remember the Father. This is knowledge. The Father says: Remember the drama cycle, the ladder and the Father. This is knowledge. Whatever Baba explains is called knowledge. He also explains the pilgrimage of remembrance to you. All of these aspects are jewels of knowledge. The things that He explains about remembrance are very good jewels."

(Sakar Murli 24-7-20)

Explanations on the murli extract for churning:

The knowledge given by Baba/God is very valuable because it enables us to enjoy wealth, status, happiness, the constant soul conscious stage and a heavenly life in the Golden Age. It is also so valuable because it enables us to enjoy peace, happiness and stability now; we can conquer depression and stress through contemplating on the knowledge. We become spiritually powerful and so we enjoy happiness to a greater extent, with time.

In the Kaliyug world, jewels are considered to be valuable. People make sure that the good jewels are always with them; they wear them at all times for good luck, good health, wealth, love, etc. So Baba has symbolically said that the knowledge, which He has given, is like jewels. You (the soul) have to keep them in your mind at all times for enjoying wealth, status, happiness, love etc. because you can claim your inheritance from God now through doing that. This means you have to keep contemplating on the knowledge. When you create thoughts on the knowledge, you keep the knowledge with you because the thoughts are created in the mind; then, the intellect takes these thoughts and puts them in the Memory Bank within the soul. Hence, these jewels remain with the soul. You have to keep creating thoughts on the knowledge to keep them in your mind. Then, it really is with you because you keep thinking about what is in your mind.

Further, the knowledge, which Baba has given, is symbolically compared to jewels because Baba's vibrations (Sounds of Silence) accompany the knowledge. When the knowledge is in our mind, Baba's sparkling pure light would also be there because the knowledge instantly connects us to Baba. So it is as if jewels are in our minds when the knowledge is in our mind.

BKs are on the 'pilgrimage of remembrance' and this includes:

1. wanting Baba to give us more jewels of knowledge.

2. wanting to understand the knowledge to a greater extent.

3. wanting to develop a loving relationship with Baba.

4. wanting to get purified now, during the Confluence Age.

5. wanting to make spiritual efforts to become spiritually powerful.

6. making spiritual efforts to transform so that the world transforms into the Golden Aged world.

BKs do not go to any play on earth during the 'pilgrimage of remembrance'. When you are on this pilgrimage, you are on a journey:

1. towards the Angelic World.

2. towards the Soul World.

3. towards the Golden Aged world.

When we say that we are on a 'pilgrimage of remembrance' we are on a metaphorical journey that begins with the journey inwards (seeing the self as the soul) and then it continues with the journey upwards towards Baba.

A pilgrimage is for spiritual or religious development. Our 'pilgrimage of remembrance' involves remembering Baba and contemplating on the jewels of knowledge, which He has given, for our spiritual development. When you remember Baba or the knowledge, your intellect flies to the Angelic World so as to be with Baba. You experience yourself as a soul or an angel, through doing this. You also begin to understand that we are all souls. You understand that Time flow in a cyclic manner and that we have been losing spiritual strength as we walked down the World Ladder. You will know that you can take a high jump now to the top of the World Ladder through spiritual effort making.

As you become spiritually more powerful, through spiritual effort making, you are getting closer to Baba. Hence, you will be closer to Baba on the journey back to the Soul World. Thus, it is as if we are on the journey back to the Soul World now, as we keep making spiritual efforts. If you get close to Baba, you will remain close to Him in the Soul World.

Our spiritual effort making now is for our journey back Home, to the Soul World. We have to purify ourselves now so that we do not experience pain (during the purification process) just before we are taken back Home. When we are purified now, we experience bliss because we are filled with Baba's pure divine vibrations as we are purified.

As you keep transforming into the divine state, you get closer to your perfect Golden Aged self. You will have experiences of being the pure divine soul. Then, when the Golden Aged world materialises, some walk into the Golden Age while you will take your next birth there. So we are on our way to our Golden Aged world through our spiritual effort making.

The 'pilgrimage of remembrance' involves doing everything which Baba has instructed us to do. Those who live outside the Brahma Kumaris, have to adopt and adjust with the ways of the non-BKs.

They have to do this because it involves using the Power to Adopt and Adjust. This power is so important that it is taught as one of the 8 powers during the BK 7 days course. As you adopt and adjust, remember that you are doing what Baba is teaching you to do and this itself keeps you on the 'pilgrimage of remembrance'. You will be able to easily do this the whole day, at your work place, at home, etc. If you did it, you have been on the 'pilgrimage of remembrance' the whole day.

If you keep remembering Baba and the jewels of knowledge which Baba gives, you will become spiritually powerful. Thus, with time, you will have more and more control over your mind, emotions, thoughts and actions. You (the soul) will also begin to glow like a beautiful diamond.

Chapter 13: Avyakt Murli on Churning Knowledge

Further down, are the words from the avyakt murli that was spoken by Bapdada on 10th January, 1988. BabDada refers to 'God and angelic Brahma Baba' when they enter the physical body of Dadi Gulzar to give teachings which are known as avyakt murlis. God (Shiv Baba) uses angelic Brahma Baba and Dadi Gulzar's physical body to give the avyakt murlis. In the murli that was spoken on 10th January 1988 (which is hereafter referred to as 'this murli'), Baba is explaining on how one should be churning the knowledge.

In this murli, God is referred to as the JewelMerchant Father because He is our Father and He is also giving us the jewels of knowledge. A merchant is one who gives something in return for something else. God is referred to as a JewelMerchant because we have to do the following so as to receive the knowledge as 'jewels' from Him:

1. we must accept the knowledge, with faith that it is from God, and

2. we should have the intention to remain linked to God through receiving, and contemplating on, the knowledge.

As reflected in this murli, God sees us as His invaluable jewels because:

1. each soul will be a sparkling point of light (looking like a sparkling jewel) when we are in God's presence.

2. when God sees us as that, we easily attain a high stage where we will be sparkling.

3. God is reminding us of our aim which should be to constantly remain in the high stage where we (the souls) will be sparkling.

In this murli, Baba informs us that He has given us numerous jewels of knowledge, and that each jewel of knowledge is invaluable. We use these jewels when we churn the knowledge. Then, when our stage is high due to the churning, Baba gives us a better understanding on the knowledge, i.e. we receive more knowledge. Thus, these jewels continue increasing within us, as we keep churning the knowledge.

In addition, when we constantly remember the knowledge, the knowledge goes on increasing within the soul because the intellect keeps taking what is remembered between the mind and the memory bank. Since new impressions (of the knowledge) are created when we remember the knowledge, and these new impressions are also stored in the memory bank, the jewels of knowledge continuously increase within the soul.

In this murli, Baba also talks about how we should be using the jewels of knowledge in all our actions and in all situations, i.e. we should use the knowledge in a practical way in our life. We use this knowledge in a practical way, through remembering God and churning the knowledge:

1. while we are in adverse situations.

2. while we do everything, as we live our lives.

No adverse situation can affect us badly:

1. when our stage is high.

2. if we are using the knowledge accurately.

Through remembering the correct points of knowledge at relevant times, you will be able to use the knowledge as a weapon to remain victorious over the vices. For example:

1. Whenever you face an adverse situation where you need to use the powers, remember the knowledge about how to use the eight powers, the knowledge about the original qualities of the soul being the virtues and powers, the knowledge about how God is an Ocean of

Powers and Virtues, etc. Then, emerge the relevant powers and virtues, while remembering Baba, so that you can handle the situation. There are eight significant powers which you can use to manage the various kinds of situations that you face in life. These eight powers are the Power to Accommodate, Power of Tolerate, Power to pack up, Power to Face, Power to Discriminate, Power to Judge, Power to co-operate & Power to Withdraw. If you normally find it very difficult to face a problematic situation or person, emerge the Power to Face from within and also absorb the Power to Face from God so that you will be able to face the problem/person. Accumulate all your other powers in this way also. As you unceasingly use these powers, they become stronger in you. You have to develop these powers so as to manage situations well. Make sure that you are using the relevant powers, while carrying out all actions, through maintaining a high stage. When your spiritual stage is high, you will know how to cope with every challenge and how to live well in every situation through using the powers properly. If you constantly use these eight powers, you learn the skill of applying the right power at the right time and in the right situation. As you use the powers, have faith that God is taking care of everything so as to make sure that you continuously get a lot of help from Him. There are more explanations on how to use the powers in my other books where the murli extracts are explained.

2. If you have done a wrong and feel very bad about it, forgive yourself; do not let it slowly destroy you. Always remember that everything happens as per the World Drama. Baba has given us knowledge about the World Drama; remember this knowledge. The wrong, which you had done, was something that had to happen, as per the World Drama, so it had happened. Don't evaluate whether the wrong will have any good consequences. Just have faith that whatever had happened was for the good. As per the BK knowledge, bad karmic accounts are settled through bad incidences. Since something got settled in your life (through that bad incidence), something good has

come out of it, i.e. you have already settled a bad karmic account. However, persistently make spiritual efforts so that you can get the karmic accounts burnt off instead of settling it. The bad that has happened is also something good because it gave you a good test paper. Since you had failed the test paper by doing the bad act, you will know that you need to make more spiritual efforts. If you are able to maintain a high stage whenever you remember the wrong which you did, you are passing each of these test papers. Facing test papers make you spiritually powerful. Therefore, be happy that you have test papers to keep testing if you are in a powerful stage. Ceaselessly make spiritual efforts to maintain the powerful stage so that you also do **not** feel bad when anyone tries to blame you for the wrong. These are also good test papers. In addition, make it clear to yourself that the vices were in control when the bad act was done by you; so you were not responsible for the bad act. Baba has told us that all souls are in the spiritually weak state by the end of the Cycle. Thus, it is easy for the vices to take control and make you do bad things. Since you were not making spiritual efforts at the time when you did the wrongful act, you were in a weak state; consequently, the vices had taken control to do the wrong thing. Go on reminding yourself that you must constantly make spiritual efforts to remain in the powerful state so that you do not do anything bad again. Have the aim to stay victorious in the battle against the vices.

3. If one sees the spouse talking to someone of the opposite sex, one can become jealous if one allows the vices to emerge and take control. To make sure that the vices do not take control, one has to remember that all souls are brothers; one should remember that even the soul in the spouse and the soul within the other person (who the spouse is talking too) are both one's brothers. You can also use these points of knowledge if it upsets you to see someone you know talking to someone else. You should remember that we are just playing roles in the World Drama and that you have to play your part well by not

allowing the vices to emerge (to make you possessive and/or jealous). See what is happening as a good test paper that is testing to see if you see everyone as souls, who are your brothers, while you also maintain a high stage. You should remember that you belong to God, and you should immediately turn your attention to God when you are faced with such situations.

The above are some examples of how you use the knowledge in a practical way, when you face adverse situations. More examples can be found in my other books which are involved with explaining the murli extracts. Actually, while your stage is high, God will be guiding you on how to use the knowledge to help yourself, when you face test papers. You get His assistance when you remember Him and churn the knowledge.

When you make spiritual efforts through churning the knowledge, you:

1. dive into the depths of the Ocean of Knowledge (God), and
2. go into the depths of each jewel.

As a consequence, you will:

1. understand the significance of each point of knowledge.
2. enjoy the intoxicating high stage.
3. understand when and how you should use the knowledge, which you are churning on.

When there is a lot of knowledge accumulated within the memory bank, the intellect can easily bring the knowledge into the mind whenever you face adverse situations. This will help you to remain in a high stage when you face an adverse situation. Hence, diligently churn the knowledge to accumulate it within you.

When you are in an adverse situation, you will have to make more spiritual efforts to make sure that you do not lose your high stage. Since you repeatedly remember the knowledge, the knowledge continues to increase to a great extent within you. In the future, this will make it easier for you to 'face adverse situations without losing your high stage'.

You imbibe the knowledge when you:

1. carry on filling yourselves with the knowledge, and

2. keep using the knowledge in a practical way in your life.

When you imbibe the knowledge:

1. you are linked to God.

2 you easily attain a high stage, and you can maintain this high stage even when you face adverse situations.

3. you have experiences. These experiences will also keep influencing you to remain in a high stage.

4. the knowledge becomes a part of you, influencing your character, how you handle everything, etc.

5. you accumulate virtues and powers since you are linked to God. These virtues and powers also become a part of you. When you persistently use these virtues and powers, as you face adverse situations, they accumulate further. The accumulated virtues and virtues will easily emerge to help you successfully deal with problems, etc.

All the above will help you to deal with negative situations efficiently.

Each jewel of knowledge is very, very valuable because when you churn the knowledge:

1. it enables you to link yourself to God and become spiritually powerful.

2. it enables you to transform into the pure, divine state.

3. it helps to give you power when you are in adverse situations or if you are faced with obstacles. It is able to empower you because God's vibrations accompany the knowledge; this is also why the knowledge links you to God.

If you churn constantly, you will be able to use each point of knowledge when it is needed; if not, when you are in a situation where you need it, you will not:

1. remember the knowledge.

2. know which murli point to use.

3. know how to use a murli point.

After receiving the knowledge and accepting it, if you do not repeatedly remember the knowledge and inculcate/imbibe it as you live your live, you will find it very difficult to experience 'happiness, joy, power, peace and a stage free from obstacles'. You should churn the knowledge with diligence, as you carry out all activities so as to continuously experience 'happiness, joy, power, peace and a stage free from obstacles'. The vices will not be able to put obstacles in your mind when your stage is high.

One lacks churning power when one knows the knowledge but does not churn consistently so as to inculcate/absorb the knowledge. Those who churn have to also use the knowledge, while carrying out all their daily tasks, as they live their lives, i.e. the knowledge has to become part of their life. If the knowledge is stored in the memory bank by the intellect, and it is not re-emerged into the mind to use as one lives one's life:

1. the knowledge will not increase within the soul.

2. the knowledge is not properly imbibed.

3. one is not becoming spiritually powerful.

The jewels of knowledge will only give great joy when it is used to keep one in a high stage, no matter what kind of situation one is faced with. One becomes spiritually very powerful, when one continually enjoys a high stage while facing adverse situations, because one is intensely making spiritual efforts to remain in control in such situations. The more the knowledge is used in adverse situations, the more the accumulation of power within the self. In such situations:

1. knowledge is the power that enables one to stay linked to God.

2. knowledge is an elevated weapon for fighting the battle against the vices. A weapon is of no use if it is not used when it should be used.

It is only when you face test papers in life that you will know if you have churned accurately or not because if you fail the test paper, and the vices are in control, there is something wrong with the way you were making spiritual efforts. If you were churning properly, you will be able to conquer the vices with ease (without labour and waste). Test papers enable you to use what you have, and you will have the practice of using it.

In this murli, Baba mentions how we are numberwise. Basically, this is referring to how the more powerful souls are further ahead in the race of spiritual effort making. The more powerful one is, the easier it is for one to:

1. use the knowledge in a practical way, as one lives one's life, so that one remains in a spiritually powerful stage.

2. use the knowledge to accumulate further knowledge.

In this murli, Baba says that we should not be careless like Kumbhakarna. In the Ramayana, Kumbhakarna (who is the younger brother of Ravana) is portrayed as sleeping for unusually long periods of time, and it is difficult for him to wake up. This myth was created by the deity souls, during the Copper Age, based on memories of what was happening during the Confluence Age. Kumbhakarna represents one who is sleeping instead of being in the awakened state through having received this knowledge. Instead of being alert and ready with the knowledge (as weapons) to fight the vices, one should not be careless thinking that when the vices come, one will make spiritual efforts. One must persistently make spiritual efforts so that when one faces an adverse situation, one will be equipped with the weapons (knowledge) to make sure that the vices are not victorious over one. One should not be sleeping instead of preparing in advance through churning the knowledge.

Churn on the different murli points, every day, to increase your power of churning. Make sure that you have experiences so that you stay interested in the knowledge. To have experiences, you must intensely churn the knowledge with faith that it keeps you linked to God. While you repeatedly churn the knowledge, you experience it in a practical way through blissful experiences. These experiences also become a part of you. When memories of these experiences emerge, you will attain and remain in a high stage. Hence, you can easily face adverse situation.

You should also experience the knowledge-full, powerful stage through being a swadarshan-chakradhari (spinner of the discus of self-realisation). You spin the discus of self-realisation when you think of how you (the soul) take many births during each Cycle (from the beginning of the Golden Age until the end of the Iron Age) and then take this spiritual birth during the Confluence Age. When you endlessly remember this, you will attain a high stage and experience yourself as the powerful soul. When you are in this powerful stage, you are in the:

1. seed stage.
2. soul conscious stage.

While performing mundane actions, do not allow the intellect to be filled with mundane, ordinary thoughts. Instead, maintain a powerful stage through powerful remembrance. You should try your best to 'perform all your actions while you are in a high stage'. This should be the aim of all spiritual effort makers. Therefore, you should try to achieve this aim. When you do actions/karma while in a high stage, you are a karma yogi. Don't just perform karma/actions; be a karma yogi. A karma yogi is one who does actions while in remembrance of Baba.

The following are four things which BK spiritual effort makers must give importance to, on a daily basis, for living a spiritual life based on Baba's teaching:

1. gyan (knowledge). One has to study the knowledge, daily. This study involves churning the knowledge to become spiritually powerful. Through this study, one also learns to see events, situations and circumstances as opportunities to apply the teachings.

2. yoga (meditation / remembrance). While in yoga, the spiritual effort maker will be having a direct link to God (to draw power from God) so as to build resilience and spiritual capacity.

3. dharna (inculcation of divine virtues). One must make sure that one inculcates the divine virtues so that one changes oneself. Inculcation of divine virtues includes the elimination of the vices through one's yoga with God. Every day, one should use one's time to consciously develop one's character (to become virtuous) while also making sure that negativity and the vices are eliminated. Through concentration on the soul and on God (as the Supreme Soul), one inculcates divine virtues and powers because one will be absorbing the divine virtues and powers from God, and one's ordinary virtues will be empowered to become divine virtues. One should have the awareness that one is the soul whose original qualities are the divine virtues and powers. One should continuously carry out all activities while in this awareness so that the virtues and powers keep increasing within one. As one does this, one is developing inner stability and one will have inner strength to overcome negative beliefs, thoughts etc. How one conducts oneself is a mirror reflection of one's dharna.

4. seva (service). One should find appropriate ways to use one's increasing spiritual power and understanding (which are acquired through the three aspects mentioned above) for the benefit of others. One earns a huge spiritual income through doing service.

All the above four are inter-connected and they help the spiritual effort maker to achieve the desired aims. The inculcation of divine virtues is often the toughest among all the four subjects because it includes facing difficult situations while maintaining one's yoga with God.

God is the Bestower of Knowledge because He gives this knowledge to us. When we remember/churn the knowledge, which has been given by Him, we are automatically remembering Him. If you stop remembering Baba, your spiritual energies leak away, and you lose your high spiritual stage. Make sure that this does not happen.

When you are churning intensely, the vices cannot emerge to influence you to have bad thoughts etc, i.e. you will be a conqueror of Maya (the vices). Since negativity is not there in your mind, you easily remain in the high stage where you are lost/absorbed in love. This means that you will experience a lot of love for God, and you will also experience His love.

At the end of the murli Baba says 'Achcha' which means good or okay. Then, Baba ends the murli in a very loving and empowering way. Since He sees us as His children who are powerful souls enjoying the following stages or qualities, He is enabling us to easily attain the following powerful stages/qualities:

1. knowledgeable children of the Ocean of Knowledge.

2. elevated souls who always easily become conquerors of Maya with the power to churn.

3. those who increase their practice of churning power and who experience the stage of being lost in love, i.e. those who use churning power to experience themselves as being absorbed in the Father's love.

4. those who always know the value of the jewels of knowledge.

5. those who use the power of knowledge in every action.

6. the special invaluable jewels who always remain stable in an elevated stage.

Further, Baba also gives us His love, remembrance and namaste. Namasté is actually more than a word that ends the murli. It is used to:

1. reflect that God, as the Supreme Soul, recognises the souls who are before Him.

2. show that God sees and honours His children as powerful divine soul.

3. show God's gesture of love, respect, deep appreciation and remembrance.

All the above help us to attain and maintain a powerful stage. It should be noted that Baba says Namaste and not Namaskar. Namaskar is a formal expression. Namaste is an informal expression. Baba says Namaste because He is our Father and we are His children.

....

10-01-88 Om Shanti Avyakt Bapdada Madhuban

Today, the JewelMerchant Father has come to meet His invaluable jewels to see how many jewels of knowledge every elevated soul has accumulated, that is, how many jewels of knowledge you have imbibed in your practical life. Each and every jewel of knowledge is more valuable than multimillions. So, just think how many jewels of knowledge you have received from the beginning until now. The JewelMerchant Father has filled the apron of the intellect of every child with many jewels. He has given all the children equal jewels of knowledge at the same time. However, the more you use these jewels of knowledge for yourself and for others, the more these jewels continue to increase. BapDada was seeing that although the Father has given equally to all the children, some children have increased their jewels, whereas others have not. Some are full, overflowing, some have unlimited treasures, some are using them according to the time, some are using them for a task and are increasing them multimillionfold. Some are unable to use these jewels for a task as much as they should. This is why they are unable to understand the value of the jewels as much as they should. Your intellect has imbibed what you have received, but you are unable to experience the attainment of happiness, joy, power, peace and a stage free from obstacles that you should have by using them. The reason for this is lack of churning power, because to churn means to put into your life, to imbibe it. Not to churn means just to imbibe in your intellect. The former use these for every task and in every action of their life, whether it is for the self or for others. The latter simply remember these with their intellect, that is, they imbibe them in their intellect.

For instance, when you keep a physical treasure locked up in your safe and you don't use it at the right time or all the time, you don't have the experience of happiness, but you just have the reassurance in your heart that you have that treasure. Neither will it increase nor will you have an experience. In the same way, if you have just imbibed the jewels of knowledge in your intellect, if you just remember them and repeat them in words saying that the point is very good, then, for a short time you have good intoxication of that good point. However, you have to put these jewels of knowledge into your practical life and into every action because knowledge is not only jewels, but knowledge is enlightenment and knowledge is also power. Therefore, if you don't use them in action with this method, neither do they increase nor is there any experience. Knowledge is a study and it is also an elevated weapon for battling. This is the value of knowledge. To know their value means to use them for a task and the more you use them for a task, the more you continue to experience power. For instance, when you don't use a weapon according to the time, then that weapon becomes useless, that is, it no longer has that much value. Knowledge is also a weapon, but, if at the time of becoming a conqueror of Maya you don't use the weapon, then you reduce its value because you didn't take its benefit. To take the benefit of something means to keep its value. You all have jewels of knowledge because you all have a right, but you are numberwise in being full. You were told that the main reason is a lack of the power of churning.

Churning power is the basis to experience the Father's treasures to be your own. Just as physical food when digested becomes blood, because food is separate, but when you digest it, it then takes the form of blood. In the same way, with churning power, you experience the Father's treasures to be your own; you experience them as a right and as your treasure. Previously too, BapDada has been saying that only when you grind your own ingredients will you feel that intoxication. That is, by using the Father's treasures with your churning power, experience

attainment and your intoxication will rise. At the time of listening to
Baba you have intoxication, but why does it not remain all the time?
The reason is that you have not made them your own with churning
power. Churning power means to go to the bottom of the ocean, to
be introverted and go into the depth of every jewel of knowledge. You
mustn't just repeat them, but what is the significance of every point,
and at what time and with what method must I use every point, and
with what method must I use every point for the service of others.
So listen to every point and think about these four things. Together
with churning, also go into the sweetness of that secret, become lost
in the experience of intoxication. Use these at the time of the different
obstacles from Maya or when you have different problems of nature:
according to the situations or according to the obstacles, whatever
points I churned, will these jewels of knowledge make me or can they
make me a conqueror of Maya? Did that happen practically? That is,
did you become a conqueror of Maya? Or, is it that you thought that
you would become a conqueror of Maya, but instead you had to labour
or your time was wasted? This proves that the method was not accurate,
and this is why you didn't experience success. You also need the method
and practice to use these things. Just as scientists bring very powerful
bombs. They believe that with those they will definitely be victorious.
However, if the person using those bombs doesn't know how to use
them, then even though they are powerful bombs, when they just fall
here or there, then they are wasted. What was the reason? The method
to use them was not accurate. In this way, every jewel of knowledge is
extremely valuable. Situations and obstacles cannot remain when you
have the jewels of knowledge and the power of knowledge. However,
if you don't have victory, then understand that you don't know the
method to use them accurately. Secondly, by not constantly having the
practice of churning, at the time of need, when you suddenly try to use
them, then you are deceived. You then have the carelessness that you
have the knowledge in your intellect anyway, and that you will use it at

the right time. However, you need constant practice and practice over a long period of time. Otherwise, what title will those who just think about these things receive? A kumbhakarna. What carelessness did he have? He only thought: Let them come, and then I will be victorious. So the carelessness to think that it will happen when it is time deceives you. Therefore, continue to increase churning power every day.

Whether it is the revised course or the avyakt murli that you hear every day, in order to increase churning power, imbibe one special point in your intellect every day and practise with the method of the four things that Baba told you about. While moving along, while performing every action, whether it is for yourself or an action for service, let churning take place throughout the day. Whether you are in business or you go to the office or whether you serve at a centre, whenever your intellect is a little free, repeatedly increase the practice of churning. Some work is such that while you are doing that work, you can also think about these things at the same time. It is for a very little time that you have to do work in which your intellect has to pay full attention. Otherwise, your intellect can continue to work on both things. If you fix such time in your timetable, you can find a lot of time in between. It isn't that you have to find special time to use churning power. You can do it even while walking and moving around. If you have some time in solitude, that is very good. Go into the depth of the clarification of every point; go into its expansion and you will enjoy yourself very much. But, first of all stabilise yourself in the intoxication of that point, then you won't get bored. Otherwise, you just repeat the points and you then say, "This is now done; what should I now do?"

When spinning the discus of self-realisation, some of you make me laugh: what should we think about? Our cycle finishes within five minutes! They don't know how to experience that stage and so they simply repeat the knowledge: the golden, silver, copper and iron ages, so many births, this much lifespan, this much time, that is all, and it is completed. However, to become a spinner of the discus of self-realisation means to experience a knowledgefull and powerful stage. Now practise with every point to remain stable in the intoxication of that point and to become a knower of the significance of that point of knowledge. This was one aspect of the discus of self-realisation that the Father spoke. In the same way, churn each and every point of knowledge and every now and then, practise having an experience. It should not be that you just sit there for half an hour simply churning it. Whenever you have time, let the intellect have the practice of churning. With churning power, your intellect will remain busy and you will automatically and easily become a conqueror of Maya. When Maya sees that you are busy, she automatically steps away. If Maya comes and you then have to battle to chase her away, and sometimes there is victory and sometimes there is defeat, that is effort of the crawling stage. Now is the time to make intense effort; it is the time to fly. Therefore, keep your intellect busy churning. Through this churning power, you will remain absorbed in the power of remembrance. You will easily have that experience. Churning makes you a conqueror of Maya and free from all waste thoughts. Where there is no waste and no obstacles, you automatically have a powerful stage, the stage of remaining lost in love.

Some think that they have very little of the seed stage or the stage of powerful remembrance, or that they have an experience after paying a lot of attention. You were told the reason for this last time too, that there is some leakage. The power of your intellect goes to waste. Sometimes, you will have waste thoughts and at other times you will have ordinary thoughts. To keep your intellect busy with the work that you are doing is known as having ordinary thoughts. At that time, you don't have the power of remembrance or the churning power that you should have, and you satisfy yourself by saying: today, I didn't commit any sins, I haven't had any wastage and I didn't give anyone any sorrow. However, did you have powerful thoughts, a powerful stage and powerful remembrance? If you didn't have these, that is called ordinary thoughts. You performed actions, but karma and yoga were not together. You became one who performs actions, but not one who is a karma yogi. Therefore, while performing actions, there should always be the experience of either churning power or the power of being lost in that stage. Both these powers are the basis of doing powerful service. Because those who churn have that practice they are able to create whatever stage they want whenever they want. By having a link, the leakage will end and whatever experience you want - whether it is the seed stage, or the angelic stage - you will easily be able to experience whatever stage you want. When you have awareness of knowledge, then by remembering knowledge, you automatically remember the Bestower of that Knowledge. So, do you understand how you have to churn? You were told that Baba would tell you about churning at some point. So, today, Baba has told you the method to churn. The basis of always being victorious over the obstacles of Maya and always experiencing success in service is churning power. Do you understand? Achcha.

To all the knowledgeable children of the Ocean of Knowledge, to the elevated souls who always easily become conquerors of Maya with the power to churn, to those who increase their practice of churning power and who experience the stage of being lost in love, to those who always know the value of the jewels of knowledge, to those who use the power of knowledge in every action, to the special invaluable jewels who always remain stable in an elevated stage, BapDada's love, remembrance and namaste.

Chapter 14: Conclusion

God/Baba has given us the knowledge in the murlis so that we can become spiritually powerful through churning it. When you churn this knowledge, you also enjoy numerous more benefits; for example:

1. you are in yoga with God. Hence, you receive His help and guidance.

2. you are not capable of indulging in the vices when your spiritual stage is high. You only enjoy the pure, powerful, virtuous stage.

3. your spiritual strength and purity increases. The more powerful you become, the easier it is to remain in the pure, powerful, virtuous state.

4. your karmic accounts are burnt away.

5. you become stress-free, depression-free, anxiety-free, peaceful, happy, blissful, etc.

6. you transform into the pure, divine state.

7. you have a loving relationship with God, etc.

Since the contents of this book explain the knowledge, which is in the murlis, you enjoy all the numerous benefits through churning the knowledge that is in this book. You enjoy benefits in this birth and in your future births. Thus, keep re-reading this book. Do not lose your spiritual stage if you do not understand something. Your understanding improves when you keep reading. When you read it the second time, you will understand a lot more because you already know everything that has been written in this book. Since the explanations in this book help you to understand the knowledge, which is in the murli extracts, you can easily attain a high spiritual stage through remembering what God has said in the murli extracts.

The author of this book and numerous other BKs have had lovely, blissful experiences through churning the BK Gyan. You can also have lovely experiences through churning this knowledge. So keep churning.

Chapter 15: About the Author and Further Assistance

The author of this book, Brahma Kumari Pari, has been practicing meditation since the 1970s. She was introduced to the knowledge of the Brahma Kumaris in 1994, and she has been a BK from that time. She began writing articles from 1996. Then, from 2014, she began writing books. All her articles and books are based on:

1. the BK knowledge,

2. God's guidance (through her own link to God and through others),

3. her experiences, and

4. her research.

The current book has also been written based on all the above. The explanations and practices in this book will help the readers to:

1. understand the BK knowledge,

2. churn the knowledge more efficiently.

More explanations on the BK knowledge can be found in her other books and articles. The links for these books and articles can be found at http://www.gbk-books.com.

BK Pari does not teach anyone on a 'one to one' basis because she does not have the time to do that. She prefers to use her free time to write books so that:

1. the knowledge can reach more people.

2. she can make spiritual efforts, in solitude, while she writes.

If you need **further assistance**, you can:

1. **go to one of the BK centers**. There are BK centers all over the world. All the classes are given for free by the Brahma Kumaris.

2. attend one of the free online sessions which is conducted by BKs.

3. read BK Pari's other books and articles.

4. listen to the videos which BK Pari has uploaded in YouTube (https://www.youtube.com/c/BrahmaKumariPari). For the List of Meditation Commentaries, which she has uploaded in Youtube, see http://www.gbk-books.com/affirmations.html.

5. join one of the WhatsApp or Telegram groups for BK spiritual effort making purposes.

6. read the books that have been published by the Brahma Kumaris.

7. watch the videos uploaded by the Brahma Kumaris.

It should be noted that the Brahma Kumaris is actually training their members to become a powerful gathering, so that the 900,000 most powerful souls are ready for world transformation. It is easier for them to become spiritually powerful if they are given strict disciplines (maryadas). Therefore, BKs give a lot of emphasis to all the BK Maryadas. However, there are many people who go to the BK centers to just feel peaceful, etc. and they are not interested in world transformation. So relevant classes are also given for these people; this is also what BK Pari is doing. Normally, all the maryadas are not enforced on those who are just coming to the BK centers to feel good. However, some BKs and BK centers prefer to just get involved with training souls to become part of the 'gathering of 900,000 most powerful souls'. So the maryadas are given a lot of importance in these BK centers. If you want to continue living a normal life and don't want to follow all the maryadas, go to a BK center where they don't enforce all the maryadas.

There are powerful vibrations in the BK centers and you can take advantage of that through going to the BK centers and sitting in that environment while you practice the knowledge in this book. God's powerful vibrations, which are constantly being emitted in the centers through the powerful BKs there, will enable you to easily attain and maintain a pure powerful stage when you are in the BK center. However, if you do not want to go to the BK center, it is alright; you can just use the knowledge given in this book, wherever you are.

Actually, you can also become one of the 900,000 powerful souls, though you do not follow all the maryadas. If you are living outside the BK center, you need not follow all the maryadas which the BKs, who live in the BKs centers, follow. Out of all the BK Maryadas, you only have to give importance to the following two most crucial Godly instructions so as to become spiritually powerful:

1. **constantly remember the Supreme Soul** who has come and given you this knowledge.

2. **constantly remember the knowledge** that has been given by the Supreme Soul.

Actually, many of the practices used in the BK centers are just part of the system of the Brahma Kumaris, for example:

1. in the BK centers, traffic control songs are played at specific times during the day. When the BKs hear the song, they have to stop whatever they are doing, and they have to sit quietly and remember Baba/God. This is like a reminder that BKs have to remember Baba. It helps them to develop the habit of remembering Baba and it makes sure that they sit in remembrance during these specific times. Some BKs try to follow this in their homes also but this is not necessary. However, while you are in the BK center, you have to sit in silence when you hear the traffic control song.

2. BKs wear white as a reminder that they have to constantly remain in the pure stage. White is seen as a sign of purity. While in the BK center, one should wear white since it is the practice in the BK centers. However, while you are outside the BK centers, you need not wear white.

3. BKs eat food which is cooked by themselves or by other powerful BKs. BKs are taught to cook food while in 'remembrance of God'

so that the food, which is being cooked, gets filled with God's pure powerful vibrations. This food will have a good influence on the soul when it is eaten. Remembering to eat food, which is cooked while in a powerful stage, is also like a reminder that one should live a pure life as a spiritual effort maker. It should remind one to continue remembering Baba. Further, BKs do not eat food cooked by people who are **not** filled with God's vibrations because the cook's weak or impure vibrations will penetrate into the food, and these can influence them badly from within. Actually, if the food has been cooked by a spiritually weak or impure soul, you can just send God's vibrations to the food (to transform the weak or impure vibrations there into the pure state) before eating it. Further, if your spiritual stage was high, God's vibrations will automatically be purifying everything that is near you. So you do not have to worry about whether there are impure vibrations in the food. The food will be purified as you eat it. If you are living outside the BK centers, it might be better not to hurt the others around you by saying that you will not eat the food that is cooked by them. Remember Baba and send His vibrations to the food which you have to eat.

4. BKs do not eat garlic and onion. In the Kaliyug world, Brahmins do not eat onion and garlic because they believe that this practice will help to keep them peaceful. Many other religious people also do not eat onions and garlic for the same reason. Actually, you will be able to link yourself to God, through just a thought based on the BK knowledge, even if you ate onions and garlics.

You do not have to quit garlic, onion, meat and sex to be a BK. If you quit these, you might find it easier to establish your link to God and remain linked to God. However, you can easily establish your link to God and remain linked to Him even if you do not quit these. You just have to make sure that your mind is in a pure, peaceful state when you make spiritual efforts. You can continue living your life, as you are doing now, while contemplating on the BK knowledge and remembering God so as to remain in yoga with God. When you contemplate on the BK knowledge and remember God, you will be linked to Him.

Most of what is used in the system of the Brahma Kumaris, as part of the BK lifestyle, is meant to help the BKs to:

1. easily remain on the pure path,
2. keep remembering that they are spiritual effort makers, and
3. constantly remember God and the knowledge given by Him.

Actually, BKs should be able to remember Baba through just constantly turning their mind towards God and His knowledge. They should not be dependent on anything external for turning their mind towards God. However, sometimes, if there is no reminder, one can forget to remember. So you can keep something around you which reminds you that you have to keep remembering Baba and the knowledge given by Him. So long as you are not indulging in the vices and are remembering 'God and the knowledge given by Him' you do not have to worry if you are not following all the practices which are used by the BKs. Just keep making spiritual efforts and you will be able to get God's help. Even if you go to the BK centers for further assistance, do not worry if you are not following all the maryadas.

BKs do not worship God to ask Him for anything because completely surrendered souls will not want anything; they will only want to remain as instruments of God. God will give them whatever they need. If those living outside the BK centers continue worshipping God for something or the other, it is considered that their time for doing worship is not over yet. These people will come to the BK center for meditation purposes and they will go to the temples for worshipping God to ask for something, etc. You can also continue the worship practices, which you are involved with now, while using the knowledge and practices in this book.

It should be noted that all religions actually teach their devotees to remain virtuous. This similarity exists among all religious practices because the original qualities of the soul are the virtues and powers. When one tries to understand the truth, one will realise that one should follow the virtuous path. The virtuous path is what you would be giving importance to while you are a BK spiritual effort maker. So long as you are using the BK knowledge to make spiritual efforts, you will be a BK spiritual effort maker and you will be getting God's assistance.

Instead of depending on other BKs for spiritual support, make your own spiritual efforts to remain pure and virtuous. Keep remembering that the original qualities of the soul are the virtues and powers, and try to give importance to this. Whenever possible, keep contemplating on the BK knowledge to establish your link to God so that you can increase the virtues and powers within you. **Keep rereading this book for further assistance to help yourself.** The more your read it, the greater the benefit.

More books will also be written by BK Pari so as to explain the contents of the murlis for churning purposes.

Other Books etc. by Brahma Kumari Pari

The following books have already been written by Brahma Kumari Pari:

1. Holographic Universe: An Introduction[1]

2. Grow Rich while Walking into the Golden Aged World (with Meditation Commentaries)[2]

3. Refresh and Heal Yourself through Meditation[3]

4. How to Think[4]

5. Recovery and Prevention: Covid-19 and other Diseases[5]

6. Overcome Depression with Ease (includes Brahma Kumaris Murli Extracts with Explanations)[6]

7. Raja Yoga Meditation for Remaining Free from Stress, Low Moods and Depression (includes Brahma Kumaris Murli Extracts with Explanations)[7]

NB: BK Pari's latest books/eBooks can be found in her List of Books (see http://www.gbk-books.com/list-of-books.html). BK Pari's articles can be read for free at: http://list-of-articles.brahmakumari.net.

---

1. http://www.gbk-books.com/book-1.html

2. http://www.gbk-books.com/book-2.html

3. http://www.gbk-books.com/book-3.html

4. http://www.gbk-books.com/book---how-to-think.html

5. http://www.gbk-books.com/book-5---healing-covid.html

6. http://www.gbk-books.com/book-6---overcome-depression.html

7. http://www.gbk-books.com/book-7---free-from-stress--low-moods-and-depression.html

Brahma Kumari Pari is also uploading meditation commentaries which you can hear for churning on the BK knowledge. Brahma Kumari Pari's 'List of Affirmations and Meditation Commentaries' can be found at: http://www.gbk-books.com/affirmations.html